THE SWIM MASTERY WAY

TRACEY BAUMANN
AND EMMA LEVY

The SwimMastery Way © Tracey Baumann and Emma Levy 2024

ISBN: 978-1-923122-28-4 (paperback)

All rights reserved. No part of this publication may be reproduced, stored in a retrieval system, or transmitted in any form or by any means electronic, mechanical, photocopying, recording, or otherwise, without the prior written permission of the author.

Published in Australia by Tracey Baumann and Emma Levy and InHouse Publishing.
www.inhousepublishing.com.au

 A catalogue record for this book is available from the National Library of Australia

Who we are and why we wrote this book

Tracey Baumann

I have no recollection of not being able to swim. Having grown up in Zimbabwe it is something I learnt at a very early age, and I then went on to train competitively both in my school team and clubs. Swim training was a huge part of my life, always outdoors. In those days we had no goggles, and I think at one particular point in my school career, I even had the privilege of wearing a cloth swimsuit, which I can assure you was very fetching. We would train most of the year, even in the colder months in unheated pools. And despite having swum in indoor and heated pools for more of my life than not, the first thought that still comes to mind all these years later is the crystal clear, freezing water hitting my skin as I dived in. And as a child growing up if I wasn't swim training I was playing with my friends in the swimming pool in the backyard. Endless hours of Marco Polo, races, seeing who could make the biggest splash with their bomb, and diving and jumping. I now shudder at the thought of these activities; they were way too dangerous for a pool that small and shallow. I loved the water then, and I love the water now, so I made it my vocation and have never looked back.

I began swim coaching in 1999, in Germany, at our local leisure centre. At that time I had no qualifications, and was just assisting a well-known coach in the area. It was then that I recognised my love for teaching movement. I went on to run some baby and toddler gymnastics classes (gymnastics being my other love), and I got such a buzz from working with the big groups, the planning of the sessions, the layout of the equipment, and seeing the joy on the faces of the children and parents; even having to sing German nursery rhymes was part of the pleasure (probably more for me than anyone having to listen to my voice). I had definitely discovered what I wanted to do with my life. I then moved to the United Kingdom with my family, and attained the relevant qualifications so I could teach swimming.

I began teaching mostly children in large groups, in local leisure centres. This was a great learning curve for me, terrifying at times, very rewarding and I won't lie, quite stressful. Although it was rewarding, I did not find it enjoyable. It became a job to go to rather than something to look forward to, and for many years I didn't understand why this was the case. I started working with more and more adults, and I found this fascinating. Most of these were private one-to-one classes, and that offered me the time to actually look at the stroke of the person in front of me, rather than just trying to tick the boxes of each of the skills that the children needed to acquire. I loved analysing the cause and effect of what the adults I was teaching were doing. It was like a puzzle to me; the only problem was that the puzzle was missing most of the pieces. I found no matter how hard I tried, with the information I had at that time I could only help some of the adults, and typically only up to a certain point.

Fortuitously, thanks to a friend who I worked with at the time, I came across some videos made by Terry Laughlin. It was the biggest lightbulb moment for me in my swimming career. Arrogantly I had thought I was a great swimmer; having swum competitively my whole life, why wouldn't I? But I was very wrong. With these new thoughts, ideas and movements in my mind I started going to the pool and literally re-learnt how to swim all four strokes, and that has been an ongoing process; one I hope never ends. It was a transformative period in my life, not only from the perspective of realising that there is so much still to be explored by experts and swimmers alike, but it was also a huge lesson in humility and understanding how it feels to learn, or rewire the brain and body for a new or improved skill.

In 2007 I went through the Total Immersion coach training program and opened my own Endless Pool™ swim studio. I had many opportunities in my early days as a Total Immersion coach to assist at workshops all over the UK. I was very fortunate to meet Terry Laughlin early in 2012 which led to me training as a coach trainer and having many opportunities to run coach training courses all over the world, often with Terry. During these years of running coach training programs, working with and learning from coaches, and then becoming a member of staff of the company, I found my love for training coaches. Training and mentoring coaches is so rewarding. Being part of a coach's journey, watching them develop into an incredible coach, and learning from them has helped me become the coach I am today.

Having now taught swimmers of all abilities, ages and with a wide array of goals in mind I have been lucky to witness some incredible journeys through the years. From someone swimming their first lap after starting out as a phobic, to the club swimmers receiving personal bests in all four strokes, to successful Channel swims, Gibraltar Strait, round Jersey, Jersey to France, the North Channel, Triple Crown winners, Apolima Strait, a record-breaking Loch Lomond Swim, a ground-breaking 66km swim in Dominica and many more.

And so began my obsession with the human body, particularly in the water. I also learnt to ask, "Why?" and started to encourage my students to ask the same thing. I learnt a lot about myself, and my learning styles, which taught me that every person we meet and every person we work with is unique. They are unique in their personalities, their mannerisms, their learning abilities and styles, what drives them and what stops them in their tracks. But I also learnt over time that every single one of them had one thing in common and that was, they were human. And whereas I know that each person has their own history, due to accidents or injuries or other life events, at the end of the day, most people have 206 bones and 360 joints and most people have a brain that can be accessed in fundamentally the same way. So started my journey of simplifying movement patterns for swimming in such a way that the human body can more easily find them. It has been a fascinating journey, exploring the natural movements the human body can access and considering how many of the positions in swimming can be thought about in slightly different ways, to allow swimmers firstly to perform movements more safely, and secondly to ensure that they are always generating forward momentum.

To understand the human body and neuroplasticity even more I attended many courses in movement development, joint mechanics, and human learning theory. Following the sad and untimely passing of Terry Laughlin in 2017, my journey with Total Immersion ended. I subsequently pulled all these threads that I had been working on in and out of the swimming pool, together to develop the SwimMastery technique.

In its first few years, SwimMastery has trained cohorts of coaches across the world. I also wanted to share the technique directly with swimmers who may or may not have access to a coach or who may prefer to work through the exercises and cues independently. I hope this book will begin to serve as that tool.

I have many people to thank who have helped me along my journey. This is by no means an exhaustive list of people who have helped me and I would like to make a special mention of the following people.

My mum, Wendy Hopcroft, for being my rock, my editor, my advisor and head cheerleader; I could not have written this book without you. Love you mom.

Emma Levy, client, friend, colleague and best thinking partner, it has been intense, fun, enriching, enlightening and rewarding. In the early stages of creating this book, due to our overlapping and complementary skill sets, and having known and worked with her since 2009 it was a no-brainer for me to ask Emma to get involved. Thank you.

Pam Adams, special friend and colleague, whose unwavering support and creative flair have brought life to many of the illustrations in this book, thank you.

Mat Hudson, a long-term friend and colleague and short-term business partner, was instrumental, in the early days, in building the SwimMastery brand and Coaching community worldwide.

Ian Smith, former Head Coach of TIUK, my coach trainer, mentor and friend. Thank you for introducing me to the word "why." Without that, I would never have started this journey.

Terry Laughlin, founder of Total Immersion: I will be forever grateful for all I learnt from Terry, and grateful that he encouraged my continued learning at every turn.

My dear friend Helen Hall: working with Helen was a big turning point for me in understanding how joints articulate, and how they affect the entire body's ability to access safe and effective movement, was a real eye-opener for me and something I look forward to diving deeper into for many, many years to come. Helen's enthusiasm and immense knowledge about human movement continue to inspire me daily.

Daniel Paasch from IPE, who opened my eyes so wide into the realms of how people learn, different learning styles, why people have blockages with learning, and how to help people to release these so they can achieve their potential.

Christa Sieber, former co-owner of RIT, taught me so much about the psychology around trauma, and about retained infant reflexes and their effects, both on people's ability to learn and on their ability to access many movement patterns in their bodies.

Euan Spence, client, friend, Masters Swimmer and my biggest teacher! Euan's incredible ability to feel and control his own body, his questions and the challenges he throws at me, have given me the opportunity to break down and examine minute parts of all the strokes. The added benefit of doing this in an Endless Pool™ with sophisticated under and overwater camera equipment with instant playback has been transformative.

To every SwimMastery Coach, being part of this Community is so rewarding; the questions and discussions over the years have certainly contributed to this book.

Big thanks to all the neverending support over the years that I have explored this swimming world to Olli, you always encouraged me to follow my heart and that is why I am lucky to do what I do today.

Thank you to my big sister Kim, friend and business advisor Melissa, soul sister Clair and "my angel" Hayley. The support has been real and appreciated.

And lastly, to my two sons, Bradley and Dylan, who have encouraged me all the way through this journey. The best part of my life though still, is being your mum.

It is thanks to all the people above that during my career I have completely reworked how I coach, both in my teaching style and in the movement patterns that I ask of swimmers. And without the swimmers I have worked with I would not be where I am today; you allowed me to try new things out and see the results; some worked and some most certainly did not, it was these failure points that gave me the greatest opportunities for growth. I have learnt as much, if not more, from observing and feeling, in my own body, the positions that did not feel right, and by performing thousands of video analyses of other swimmers, which have given me the opportunity to slow each position down to see the cause and effect. In the medium of water, there are so many opportunities for an incorrect movement to create problems as it is so unstable. Therefore, it is as important to pay as much attention to minimising these as it is to pay attention to the correct movements. And therefore, *the biggest thanks need to go to all the swimmers who have worked with me over all these years.*

Emma Levy

Like Tracey, I began life as a competitive club swimmer. Into my teens I swam at county level in the UK, and life largely consisted of being driven around town with my friends from one pool to another for several pool sessions a day, by a support squad of equally committed parents. I always assumed that I would continue to swim forever, and after I stopped swimming competitively I continued to swim regularly, and was inspired by Masters swimmers many years my senior who continued to perform at a high level.

That assumption was challenged some years later when, after training for and participating in triathlons for several years, I experienced a number of injuries that abruptly stopped me swimming, cycling, and running. This had a huge negative impact on my mental health. After several years of treatment across a number of joints that culminated in shoulder surgery, I still could not swim without agonising pain after just one length. That was when I knew I had to make dramatic changes to my technique if I was to swim again, and that was when I found Tracey. Under Tracey's guidance I gradually developed new skills, across all four strokes, that were effective, efficient, and above all safe for my joints. Over the years since then, I have returned to regular swimming, in the pool and open water, as well as cycling and running, and my belief that my own swimming will continue as I age has been restored.

At a particularly inspiring session with Tracey, I realised I could marry my personal and professional interests by becoming a swim coach. I had been working for many years in education and training, in a number of different contexts. At that point I was working as an Improvement Advisor, supporting healthcare workers with skills to manage their own improvement projects. I was excited at the prospect of applying my training, coaching, and improvement science skills to swimming.

Since becoming a swim coach, I have found that my early education in psychology and medical sciences has provided a helpful foundation for ongoing learning to become a better coach. Above all I am fascinated by the potential of the human mind and body to develop and adapt across the lifespan, and continue to build my own knowledge and skills in movement development, joint mechanics, nervous system regulation, breathing, and prevention and management of persisting pain. I aim to support people to develop strategies to adapt their physiology and anatomy to find safety, comfort and control to optimise performance and resilience.

This book is one means to reach swimmers with a toolkit they can draw on to improve their swimming performance, whatever their specific goals. It has been a privilege to work with Tracey as her thinking partner in its development.

How to use this book

Who is this book for?

This book is for almost anyone who wants to improve their freestyle.

There are two exceptions. Firstly, elite swimmers. We outline some of the differences in the challenges that the rest of us face compared with elite swimmers, and why we need to work on our stroke technique in different ways, in Chapter 10: Catch. Secondly, people who would like to learn to swim but first need to build their confidence in the water. They may have experienced a traumatic incident earlier in life, or lack confidence around water or consider themselves to have a phobia for some other reason. Whatever the cause of the lack of confidence (and you might not realise that this applies to you until you make your first attempts to swim), it's important to resolve any water-related trauma and build your confidence in the water before embarking on the activities in this book.

Everyone else who would like to improve their freestyle will benefit from understanding and applying the principles in this book. You may be a highly competent and experienced swimmer setting yourself challenges to perform at higher levels in terms of distance or speed. You may be relatively new to swimming and want to swim more efficiently for your general physical and mental wellbeing. You may be an open water 'dipper' who loves the water and is looking for new ways to enjoy it. You may have historical or current musculoskeletal injuries, associated with swimming or other activities, and be looking for changes that you can make to your stroke that will be safer for your joints and muscles. These are just some of the possible motivations that have led you to read this book.

We are addressing the book to 'you', assuming that you are a swimmer. However, it also has much to offer others with an interest in swimming who are supporting others, for example swim coaches or parents of children learning to swim or swimming competitively.

Do you also want to improve your other strokes? While this book is specifically about freestyle, the principles of joint mechanics and the physics of how the human body moves through water are also applicable to backstroke, breaststroke, and butterfly. The SwimMastery Way for swimming those strokes will be the subject of future books.

Where should you start?

We recommend that you start with Chapter 1 and continue in the sequence that the chapters are presented. However, learning is never linear, so rather than reading the book straight through, we would expect you to revisit content of earlier chapters multiple times before you reach the end. You will find out more about why this is important in Chapter 2: How to Practise, in the section on Spiral Learning.

That said, everyone has preferred ways to learn, and you may find that you read the book all the way through first, before returning to earlier chapters. If you choose to do this, when you start trying out the practical activities, we recommend that you do this in the sequence that they are presented.

Practical activities

The book includes practical exercises on dry land as well as in the water. The dryland activities are important rehearsals for what you will do in the water, helping your brain to make the movements you are rehearsing more relevant in the more familiar vertical position before taking them to the horizontal and nose down in a medium we cannot survive. We label the in-water activities as 'pool' activities. Even if you are primarily an open water swimmer, we recommend that you practise new skills in a pool first. This generally provides a more suitable environment, in terms of control of water temperature, depth and availability of sides and walls to push off from, movement of the water, and etiquette and safety around other people and equipment. Above all, the more controlled environment makes it easier to attend to the specific skill that you have chosen to address in each swim, and the quality of your attention is key to creating and maintaining changes in your movement patterns. If you normally spend more time in open water, you will of course transfer the skills you have begun to explore through your earlier practice sessions in the pool, when you are next in open water.

We sometimes suggest that you make notes. This may be a mental note or a written note. However, human memory is hugely unreliable, so written notes are usually more helpful. This will accelerate your improvement by ensuring that you repeat movement patterns that are working well, and reduce potential time wasted repeating less effective positions and movement patterns. As you progress through the book you will find more and more reasons to have a waterproof notebook with you at the pool. I hope is to turn each of you into obsessive note takers by the end of this book!

The body positions and movement patterns in this book assume that you have no injuries currently restricting your movement in these areas. While the movements and exercises work with most people, we cannot take into account individual differences in movement history, injuries or abilities. You do the activities at your own risk based on your own knowledge of any musculoskeletal limitations, as well as any advice you may have received from a doctor, physiotherapist or other suitably qualified movement or healthcare practitioner. If you are at all unsure please first consult your physician.

Terminology

Whenever there is reference to anatomy or physiology we aim to use lay terms rather than scientific terms or jargon. However, as with any learning there is always some terminology relating to the subject matter that may be new. We briefly explain anatomical and other technical terms when they first arise in the text, and they are generally accompanied by images that highlight the particular aspect of the terms that are relevant to the skills and activities described.

To make the most of all the concepts explored in this book, whether your preferred route to learning is through text, images, or by immediately doing, we recommend that you take the opportunities we offer to use all 3 strategies, as the best way to make the changes in your freestyle that will lead you towards achieving your goals.

Foreword

Enveloped by the water, my mind wanders, and I reel it back in. It takes off in a new direction, and I refocus. I can do this for hours. Literally. Down rivers, across lakes, around islands, from one bit of land to another. But when I met Tracey, I was at a precarious point in my journey. As a swimmer, I wanted to swim further, but I was stymied by shoulder discomfort. As a coach, I was overwhelmed and unsure what to recommend to my swimmers when I could not swim comfortably myself.

Through the SwimMastery principles, I found my frame, struck streamline, and gathered the momentum to slip through the water in each and every stroke. Once I learned how to connect my joints, swimming became pain-free! With no medication, no injections, and no physical therapy required. Simply finding the correct body position in each and every stroke.

Through focused practice, with Tracey as my coach, I retrained my body on how to swim.

Despite being a lifelong swimmer, I started from scratch. The dryland rehearsals were curious, but finding my body in the water was even more challenging. I thought I knew how to swim, and now I was having moments where I wasn't sure. Frustrated, I envied those new to swimming because they weren't 40 years stuck in their ways like me.

Of course, the water can be startling to new swimmers. It is a sensory overload in its sensory deprivation. Some sounds are louder, while others are muted. Without goggles, our vision is blurred. We need to exhale out our nose, depriving us of smell, and close our mouths, other than for a split second when we take in air.

But like any skill, if you break it down, you can build back up. It will be no time at all before you look back and realize how far you've come. And that's the beauty of The SwimMastery Way. In swimming, the overwhelm is real. Tracey teaches us exactly where to put our focus through cues, break it down and build back up. Stick to her recommendations for the best results.

With the SwimMastery technique and principles in this book, you will learn how to connect your joints to conserve energy and reduce your chance of injury. Stop going through the motions, kicking and pulling to stay above water. Instead, pay attention to what's happening: between the walls, in each stroke; each moment.

The increased focus and attention to technique in your regular practice will result in free speed! And no need to build up meters or miles in your practice to swim further; you are always ready.

And this is how it happened for me; once I was pain-free, I wondered: how far can I go?

16km? 35km? 50km? Yes!

Not only can I swim farther, but I swim with less effort. Because I'm using my joints in the manner in which they are intended to be used, there is no pain or discomfort, not even after 25 hours of continuous swimming.

Shannon House Keegan, Marathon Swimmer

I used to lug toys to the pool to help fill the time. I would build up distance over the course of a season. Killing time in the pool with pointless sets that I made up on the fly – whatever it took to get in more yards/meters/miles.

Contents

Who we are and why we wrote this book iii
How to use this book xi
Foreword. xv

Chapter 1:	The Challenges of Swimming	1
Chapter 2:	How to Practise.	11
Chapter 3:	Air Exchange	35
Chapter 4:	Building the frame	53
Chapter 5:	Flutter	75
Chapter 6:	Streamline	89
Chapter 7:	Generating forward momentum	105
Chapter 8:	Stroke synchronisation	121
Chapter 9:	Integrated Breathing.	133
Chapter 10:	Catch	149
Chapter 11:	Two-beat leg press	175
Chapter 12:	Advanced Synchronisations	189
Chapter 13:	Speed	205
Appendix 1:	Sample Swim Session Plans	219
Appendix 2:	References.	233

Chapter 1

The Challenges of Swimming

One of the biggest questions to ask when thinking about swimming is why so many people find it such a struggle, both to learn and to do. It is human nature to apply terrestrial logic to everything we do, and this is precisely what makes swimming different - and challenging. People tend to transfer their land-based instincts to swimming, so what we often see are people relying on their limbs to get them from A to B. Whereas our priority should be to have a wonderfully connected body that moves as one unit, much like a dolphin's. This chapter looks at some of the main reasons why, as non-aquatic mammals, swimming is a counter-intuitive skill.

Overcoming instinct

Overcoming our instinct to survive at all costs is one of the main reasons why people struggle in the water, but this issue is very rarely addressed. Humans cannot survive in water; the survival instinct kicks in before we even think about what to do with our torso, head, or limbs. Our brain is very attached to being able to see the air that we breathe, so when we are face down in the water and asking ourselves to take a breath with most of our head remaining submerged, it is understandable that our brain doesn't trust that the air is there, until we teach it to. During all my years of coaching, I have recognised this survival instinct in almost every swimmer I have worked with to varying degrees. People who have swum regularly throughout their lives may be adamant that they have absolutely no fear of the water whatsoever. However, when we start working on the breathing part of the stroke, we often see signs of compensation and bracing, which indicate that the survival instinct is still very active.

To explore how we overcome these automatic physical responses to being in the water, let's consider the roles of two distinct parts of the brain: the limbic system and the neocortex. The survival instinct is located in the limbic system, which, in evolutionary terms, is one of the older parts of the brain. It determines how we respond to things emotionally. It is like a sorting house, sorting through events, scenes, and pictures and then deciding on an appropriate response. These responses are often based on past experiences or, in this instance, on the human reflex and need to breathe. The neocortex, which developed more recently in evolutionary terms, is involved in logical thinking and creativity. We cannot access the neocortex when the limbic system is active. When we are swimming, the interactions between these two parts of the brain and our sympathetic and parasympathetic nervous systems give us an opportunity to overcome instinct.

When a swimmer is in the water, and the survival instinct kicks in, the limbic system sets off the fight, flight or freeze response. This activates our sympathetic nervous system, which sends a cocktail of hormones (cortisol and adrenaline) rushing through our veins and influencing all our body's systems, including our heart rate and breathing. When we are in fight, flight or freeze mode, it is impossible for our neocortex to identify where our arms are or what our legs are doing. Once we are able to activate the parasympathetic nervous system and turn off the sympathetic nervous system, we benefit from its calming effect. This allows us to access the neocortex and take control of our body parts.

Early on in my work with clients, I address the challenge of overcoming instinct through strategies to both activate the parasympathetic nervous system and access the neocortex. This groundwork enables us to move forward with learning technique.

Only with awareness do we have any chance of changing anything; through awareness, we change our muscles' responses to our instinct to survive. For instance, if I know that my neck is tense, causing my head to be too high in the water, I am then more likely to be able to target that area and relax the neck muscles to ensure my head drops into a neutral position. For many people, that simple awareness and acceptance is enough to keep the survival instinct at bay, but for others, more work is needed. People's sense of confidence in water lies on a spectrum, with one end of the spectrum occupied by reluctant non-swimmers.

Swimming needs a connected body

The human body is made up of 360 joints that all move to varying degrees. These movements allow the body to hinge at the joints, creating disconnections. For example, at the hip joints (see Figures 1.1 and 1.2), we need the torso and legs to be in a straight line. In this example, hinging at the hip joints will cause the legs to drop. This increases the resistance of the water, which is over 800 times denser than air, against the legs. This results in the swimmer becoming fatigued, as they have to put more effort into moving forward and fighting the resistance that their disconnected bodies are causing.

Let's think about what happens to the 360 joints when we walk. Stand up and walk across to the other side of your room. As you walk, ask yourself which body part begins the movement. I ask my clients this all the time, and I get many answers. Often, they

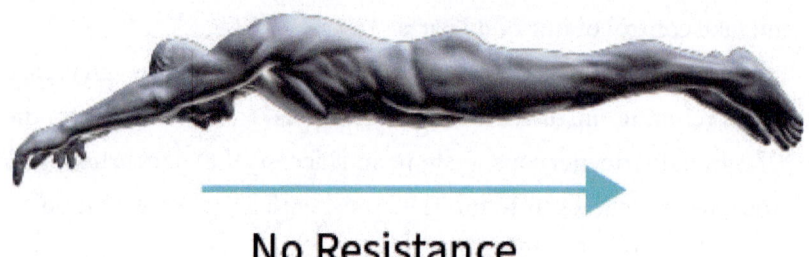

Figure 1.1: Connected at the hip.

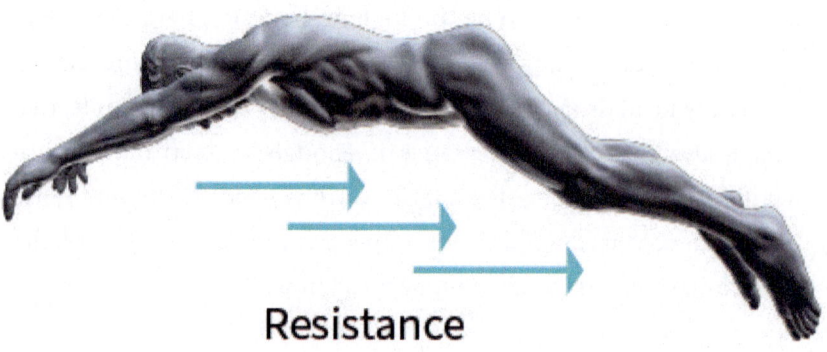

Figure 1.2: Disconnected at the hip.

say the leg or the arms. But when we really analyse and feel the movement in our bodies, it becomes very apparent that, typically, everything moves at the same time. Now, walk across your room one more time and purposefully try to use a single body part to start the movement; for example, move your arm first or try to move your pelvis first as you walk. How does that feel compared to your regular walking? Walking is a movement that you probably haven't consciously thought about in decades. When you do, it becomes self-evident that trying to isolate a single body part whilst walking feels ridiculous.

Having understood how walking is an integrated, connected movement using the whole body, we want to apply the same principle to swimming, eventually having a wonderfully connected body that all moves as one unit. When we look around the world at how swimming is typically taught and practised, we can see parts of the stroke being singled out and focused on in isolation. This creates a disconnected and mistimed stroke, very similar to the walk you have just tried. Swimmers who are singling out their limbs to swim, driving the stroke by pulling and kicking, are using less effective muscles, such as the small muscles around the shoulder joint or the very oxygen-hungry quads and hamstrings in the thighs. An even bigger problem is the injuries that can result from these movements. How often do we hear of swimmers with shoulder injuries? These injuries can be prevented by learning the safe, biomechanically correct, and efficient movements of a connected body.

So, in their efforts to move through water, humans have their own survival instinct and their own body working against them before they even begin to think about the actual mechanics of the ideal swim stroke.

Swimming is horizontal

Another challenge is that most activities that we do on land are primarily vertical and, of course, with our head out of water. In contrast, swimming is a horizontal activity carried out with our head partially submerged in water. Both of these features pose huge challenges. The human skeleton is incredible in so much that it is designed for each bone to sit on top of another bone so that we can take advantage of gravity to stand upright. The muscles can then react to support this system. However, in swimming, we no longer have the benefit of gravity holding our bones on top of each other, so we have to hold our skeleton in place. We must, therefore, take into consideration which muscles are required to keep the body connected without the benefit of gravity to help it.

Placement of the lungs

The lungs, of course, contain air and float, so having our lungs placed in the upper part of our body creates enormous balance issues.

When swimming, we have more weight behind the lungs, from the lower part of the torso to the feet, than we do in front of them. This causes a swimmer's legs to sink as the lungs and head will naturally float to the surface if we don't do anything to compensate for this discrepancy in weight.

In Figure 1.4 you can see the distance between our centre of mass, lying just beneath our naval, and our centre of buoyancy, sitting somewhere in the sternum area. This distance is quite large and causes the body to have an upward trajectory, creating

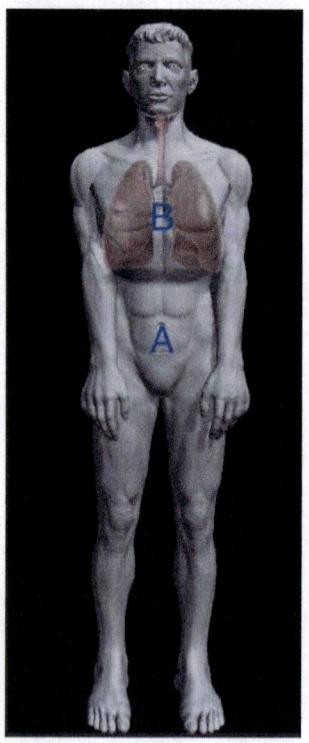

Figure 1.3: Position of the lungs
(A) Naval
(B) Sternum

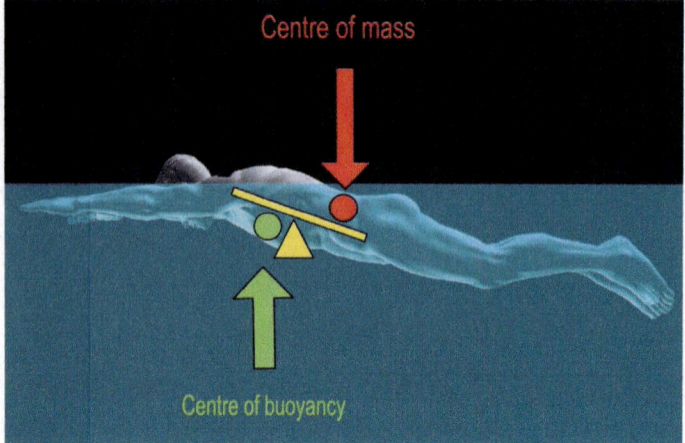

Figure 1.4: Distance between Centre of Mass and Centre of Buoyancy.

The Challenges of Swimming

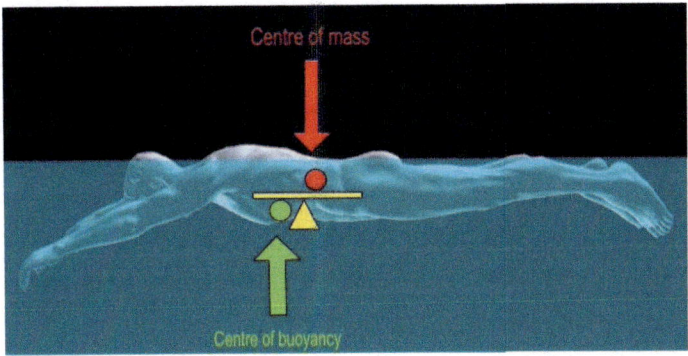

Figure 1.5: Bringing the centre of mass and centre of buoyancy closer together to attain true horizontal balance.

enormous amounts of form drag and, therefore, resistance. This is a common position we see in swimmers around the world.

Bringing the centre of mass and centre of buoyancy closer together is the only way to attain true horizontal balance in the water. We use the shifting of body parts frontwards to achieve this. For example: sliding the scapula (shoulder blade) forward, relaxing the neck muscles so the head floats, and ensuring we keep body parts forward of the lungs as best we can to help with the weight distribution. As soon as any of these body parts fall backwards, we run into the danger of the distance between the centre of mass and the centre of gravity increasing again. We then have to rely on other forces, such as pulling and kicking, to maintain that balance, resulting in increased energy use.

We can, of course, obtain horizontal balance by using the muscles in the legs and the arms, but finding true balance is much less energy-intensive and frees up the limbs to be used in more efficient ways.

Proprioception in water

While in water, another challenge that we face that is closely linked to the survival instinct referred to above, is proprioception.

To experience what proprioception is, stand up and try this: close your eyes and take your right hand and send it directly out to the side of you, palm facing downwards; then take your left hand and put your forefinger on the tip of your nose; then open your eyes and see if your right arm and your left arm are where you thought they were. That is proprioception: the sense of where parts of your body are in space, and their movement. When we immerse ourselves in water, an environment in which we cannot survive, our sense of proprioception becomes very distorted. So we have to spend some time training this sense whilst swimming. Over the years, I have asked many clients where they think their arm is, for example, at a particular phase in the stroke cycle, and have then shown them where it actually is on the video recording. Often they are surprised, if not shocked, as they find they had been completely unaware of where their arm actually was.

As your body control and awareness grows, and of course, your comfort levels, so too will your proprioception and your ability to trust that a part of your body is indeed exactly where you think it is!

The 5% rule

I often hear swimmers telling me that they can't swim because 'I'm a sinker'. I'm sure some of you reading this now are saying, yes, that's me. But in truth, most people are able to float in the water with no problems at all. As a rule of thumb, when a human body is floating in the water, approximately 95% of the body mass will be submerged and 5% of the body mass will be above the water.

This obviously varies depending on whether the swimmer is in freshwater or seawater, and of course, there will be variations depending on the body makeup, physique, muscle mass and amount of subcutaneous fat. In my 20+ years of coaching swimmers, I have in fact only ever come across two true sinkers. Despite many more claiming they were.

The Challenges of Swimming

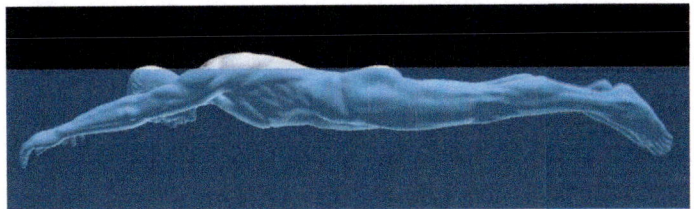

Figure 1.6: The 5% rule.

In Chapter 3 we will explore some solutions that you can try out if you think you are a sinker.

There are many other factors that make swimming very challenging for humans.

When we are on land, we know when we take a step that the ground underneath is solid and will support us, giving us an anchor for our next step. In contrast, water is an unstable medium; because it moves, and our brain tells us that we cannot use it as an anchor. However, in later chapters, we will discover different ways that we can use water as an anchor.

When we look at the neuroscience, physiology, hydrodynamics and other aspects of physics involved, it is no wonder that learning to swim correctly and efficiently requires time and the ability to recognise that because we are land-based and not aquatic mammals, the optimal way forward is to think outside the box. As coaches, we get used to saying the word "counter-intuitive".

Over the next few chapters, we will build up the stroke and your understanding of the body in an integrated way that takes into account the challenges referred to here.

Chapter 2

How to Practise

"*I want to be perfect at everything right now!*" This is a common theme that I have heard throughout the years I have spent working with swimmers. You may recognise that you could improve on part of your stroke, and, indeed, you want to make that improvement, but, like many of us, you may struggle with the discipline required to achieve it in the most efficient way.

When I begin to work with a swimmer, one of the things I say to them in their first session is that they have to be open to *learning how to learn* as well as to execute the various body positions and movements that we are looking for. It is the discipline of learning that is our greatest challenge and skill. Once we achieve this discipline, it can be applied to any area of our lives, not just swimming.

Goal-setting

There are several things to think about when we are learning a new skill. First of all, *WHY*? Why do we want to improve our swimming? This gives us a goal. We can develop these into short, medium and long-term goals, but to start with, we need to have one clear end goal. Examples of goals are anything from wanting to improve technique to using swimming to achieve fitness and well-being to more challenging goals of swimming the English Channel. Goals are very personal and a very important first step on the journey of learning.

You need a goal that answers the question '*How good, by when?*', and it must be specific. For example, instead of 'I want to swim 1000m continuously', it may be 'By July 2023, I'm going to swim 1000m continuously in the pool, at effort level 5 out of 10 with an average of 22 strokes per length'. Or, not just, 'This year I'm going to swim more freestyle outdoors instead of breaststroke', but 'By May 2023, I will immerse my face within 2 minutes of stepping into the sea, and then swim freestyle for at least 10 minutes'.

Once you have established your end goal, the next most important thing to do is to identify your starting point. You can go back to this at any time to remind yourself of where you began and is the best way of seeing your progress. It also helps you to understand the gap between where you are now and where you want to be so that your end goal is stretching - challenging, but achievable. This start point could be marked by a video analysis with a coach or a set that you swim in the pool that you make a record of, which can be compared with later repeats of the same set. It amazes me how many of my swimmers move the goalposts during their journey with me, forget where they actually started and therefore, never feel that they have progressed much. This can make the journey that much harder. So I am constantly reminding my clients of where they actually started.

This also links to the need for a goal to be time bound. Without a specific timeline, it slips by surprisingly quickly and it is easy to procrastinate or to not really apply ourselves to making the changes we want. A '*by when*' is a great motivator.

Process

> *Deliberate practice is the gold standard, the ideal to which anyone learning a skill should aspire.* (Ericsson & Pool)

Once you have set your goal, it is important to set a series of milestones you plan to achieve between now and your end goal that will assist you in achieving it. These milestones are often distance or time-based for most swimmers around the world, and there's nothing wrong with that. But it is also possible to set more subjective milestones, such as:

- I would like my air management to feel easy
- I would like to swim in open water (regardless of distance)
- I would like to leave the pool having enjoyed my set and feel as though I have improved as a swimmer

To meet our milestones, we usually need to make changes to a number of different processes. This book proposes many different processes, or tools, that swimmers can apply to support their progress towards their swimming goals. As with any toolkit, effective use of each tool requires knowledge and skill, and each swimmer will draw on the various tools at different times and work with them for the duration that gives them the best results. To get the most benefit from this book, you will work with tools one at a time, and will likely find yourself returning to some of the tools more often than others.

Learning how to learn

The hard and fast rules for becoming an expert learner are honesty, accountability and focus. The human brain is innately lazy; we all have a self-protecting survival mechanism in place. Our brains use as little capacity as they possibly can at each moment so that, should that well-known sabretooth tiger suddenly jump up behind us, we have enough brain capacity remaining to initiate the fight-flight response, and flee. I don't know about you, but I haven't seen many sabretooth tigers recently, so perhaps, nowadays, we could make our brains direct more capacity to what we want to think about; this is a conscious choice.

The key thing to remember during your entire journey of reinventing, revamping or improving your technique is that when you are not thinking about something to do with improving your swimming, your body will go into default mode, where you will simply revert to imprinting old movement patterns. Once you acknowledge this, you will make far greater progress far more quickly. Getting in the pool and swimming 2 km with no focus may feel great, will certainly make you fitter and feel more healthy, and is often great fun and very enjoyable. Because you might have gone for a swim to 'switch off', enjoy the water and get fit, for that day, the process changes from improving technique to experiencing enjoyment and well-being, and that is fine. But with no focus on your stroke during that 2 km, you will get out at the end of your swim with exactly the same technique that you started with.

I'll give you an example of a particular client of mine that I have worked with for many years. Let's call him Greg. Initially, a friend of his had brought him along to one of his lessons with me. He was very fit and had swum all his life. He had grown up in Africa and spent his entire childhood in water. He liked to swim for an hour but was feeling frustrated because he never seemed to swim further than 3 km per hour, although his aim was to swim 3.2 km in one hour by the next open water season. We began with a video analysis of his stroke. I set the pool current and started the video, and he began to swim. It was fascinating! The pool seemed to turn into a Jacuzzi, and by the end of his one minute swim, I was convinced there was more water outside of the pool than in. He was going so fast that during the swim, I had to speed up the propulsion unit of my Endless Pool several times for it to keep up with him. When Greg finished, he stood up, bright red in the face and panting but looking very pleased with himself. I then had the difficult task of analysing the stroke of a 40-something-year-old who had never considered that he may need to improve his technique. He had never known what it was like not to be able to swim; swimming was just part of who he was. Yes, he did come back for coaching! We worked on his stroke, and during our lessons (which were very enjoyable for us both), he was focused and made changes in his swimming that were visible to see on the playback video during each session. We were both delighted - until he came back the next time and proudly told me of all the distances that he had swum since our last lesson and how amazing he thought it was that he could do his early morning swims and just switch off. Needless to say, when we videoed him at the beginning of his next session, his stroke looked exactly like it did before, and we both felt the inevitable frustration. Two years later, he took part in an English Channel relay team that I had put together. He had progressed a great deal with his technique during this time, but he was no faster. His technique looked better, and it definitely felt better to him, and he was able to swim for longer and longer distances without fatigue, but the speed he was aiming for eluded him. We faced a dilemma.

He was coming to my Endless Pool™ swim studio regularly for lessons. I was giving him new tools, and he was making progress during each lesson. This was visible to me through the 4 under and over-water cameras that were displayed on a television screen. He was also increasing his speed in the lessons - I needed to increase the speed of the swim current, but this speed was not transferring into his pool or open water swimming. This conundrum continued for some time, and at each session, he would tell me how much he had enjoyed his 'practice session' that week, or morning, where he had just switched off from the world and swum 3 km in a beautiful outdoor pool near where he lived. So I asked a question - it was probably the question that changed everything for him. I asked, "When you feel you have switched off and are just enjoying not thinking about anything during your 3 km swim, are you *actually* not thinking about anything?" He looked at me quizzically for a while, not really understanding what I had asked, and then answered, "Absolutely, I don't think about anything". I questioned him further, "Are you sure?" He thought for a little while longer, then I suddenly saw his face change with realisation, and he said, "No, I *do* think about things. I think about work or my wife and children, or about the bike ride that I need to do that evening." This was an important insight for him. It is true that, as humans,, we are actually always thinking. I offered him an idea that I hoped would help overcome his resistance to focusing on technique cues. I suggested that, for just 15 minutes of his hour swim, he focus on three points that we had worked on during the lesson. With some resistance, he accepted the challenge.

Up until this point, he had been swimming about 2.9 to 3 km an hour, a barrier he was desperate to get past, but couldn't. I sent him away that day with clear guidance on how to think about his three things for that 15 minute period during his next hour's swim. Over the following few months, he would return for lessons and report back on his level of success in focusing for the 15 minute periods. He admitted that, at first, it was very challenging, and he would often lose focus during one length and have to regain focus at the start of the next. Slowly but surely, he was able to stay focused for the 15 minutes, at which point we increased the attention goal to half an hour. He incrementally increased the length of the focus period in the pool over the next six months during the cold water season, when he was not able to do any great distance in open water due to the cold. His stroke was now visibly changing when he came for each lesson; it was clear to see his focus had improved, and he was now solidly imprinting the thought processes between lessons. When the next open water season began, he set off for a swim, and afterwards, he sent me a text saying that, for the first time in his life, he had swum 3.2 km in one hour. He was delighted, and so was I. What had made all the difference to his swimming and helped him achieve his goal was his understanding that I could give him the tools, but he had to focus on deliberately using them during his practice swims. He still loves swimming, still focuses, still wants to improve, and is swimming faster and longer distances each year.

When we are attempting to learn something new, whether it is in the field of movement, thinking or attitudes and emotions, it is only possible if we are completely focused on one single new movement pattern at any one moment. The reason for this is that, until a movement pattern is embedded, we can only focus on that one thing. Let's start with some maths.

2 x 2 = ?

No doubt you very quickly answered with 4.

What about 157 x 563?

Did you find yourself reaching for pen and paper?

You could only answer this by giving it your full attention, whereas the answer to 2 x 2 is an automatic response. Until a new movement pattern is automated in this way, we need to be disciplined in our attention to the specifics of this pattern. We cannot focus on two new things at a time.

As an example, if I ask you to focus on relaxing the muscles in the back of your neck and I ask you to bubble out through your nose, your focus will immediately go to your neck, and you will relax it, but almost certainly, to begin with, the bubbles out through your nose will stop. When you focus on the bubbles, your neck may not be relaxed, and you will not have awareness of it. Once each of these single thought processes and movements have been imprinted and moved into long-term memory in the cerebellum and a movement pattern has been practised enough and ingrained as a neurological pathway, it will continue to happen when we are not thinking about it. We are striving for that well-known progression from 'unconscious incompetence' to 'conscious incompetence' to 'conscious competence' and then on to 'unconscious competence'. We are working with the brain first to make it aware of what is going on, albeit incorrectly; then being able to achieve the new skill through conscious focus, then achieving the desired result of the movement pattern being imprinted and ingrained, requiring no conscious thought process. This is the journey, and it is a journey that cannot be bypassed: there are simply zero shortcuts.

Another client I have worked with for many years was at the other end of the spectrum regarding focus and practice. Yvonne was a competitive swimmer in her youth, swimming all four strokes many times a week with a swimming club. She did the usual pounding up and down the pool, spending hours covering many kilometres a week. Yvonne came to me in 2009 with her shoulder injured. She returned to swimming after a break of several years and immediately felt pain when swimming in her local pool. Yvonne is a teacher and also works in project management. She is very detail-oriented and focused in her approach to both life and work, and analysis, and being able to quantify progress, are very important to her. I encourage all my students to challenge what I say to them and to ask questions until they fully understand what it is I'm asking them to do and why. It is only then that I can expect them to go away and practise using the tools that I give them. Yvonne regularly challenged me, asking many questions and, through this, played a big role in my own personal growth as a coach and my understanding of the stroke. I am very grateful to her for this. Her love of detail and her focus made Yvonne a dream client for a coach. We would work on several parts of the stroke in her lessons, chat about them, analyse them, and understand them. I would give her several tools to take away with her, and Yvonne would go away and practice. Diligently. Exactly. Yvonne would be so focused on her swimming and putting the tools that we had worked on into her stroke that her shoulder pain was soon a thing of the past, and her freestyle stroke looked amazing.

The only trouble was Yvonne had got slower - a lot slower. Her technique was improving considerably, her pain had gone, and her focus was razor-sharp, but none of this was transferring into significant forward momentum in her actual swimming. Yvonne and I discussed this and considered the possibility that the intense focus and need to ensure that every position was being hit correctly were hindering her ability to connect with the water and channel her energy forward. All her attention was on exact positions and none on why she had actually started this journey, which was to be able to swim as she did before, with no pain. We decided to change tactics a little. We still focused on technique, but we started to use this focus to channel her energy forward - to focus on the learnt technique moving her forward through the water. It was an amazing learning opportunity for me as a coach to work out and understand how these two things are mutually dependent. With no feeling of connection with the water, we are not able to hit the positions optimally, and with no technique in place, we are not able to feel a connection with the water. This changed the way I coached people. From then on, I introduced this duality from the first coaching session with clients - it was all about technique **and** how that technique can aid you in moving forward in the water.

Our brains will switch off at the drop of a hat; they are designed to do that. So I needed to explore whether the way Yvonne was practising the tools I was teaching her was having that effect on her brain. We also discussed how she was focussing in the pool. She had created a program to work on a single element of her stroke for a month, albeit she was varying the detail of the 3 to 4 weekly sessions, but they would all follow the same theme. There are many excellent books available that talk about brain plasticity and how the brain works, which explain that if we do one thing repeatedly for too long, the brain will switch off. I suggested to Yvonne that she change her program to work on three themes, or elements, per month, giving her greater variety and more opportunity to ensure that other aspects of the stroke were improving at the same time. But, most importantly, this would keep her brain more engaged. We still wanted to maintain the intense focus, but we wanted to vary that focus.

Another trick to use to keep the brain engaged is to do something different from what you normally do. For example, if you normally push off from the wall and execute your first stroke with your right arm, try pushing off the wall and executing your first stroke with your left arm. Like with the 2 x 2 = 4 example (where your brain has learnt tables by rote), when you always start with the same arm, the brain is automated to 'swimming' in a habitual way; therefore, there is no need for it to be engaged. But when you start off with the other arm, the brain becomes alert, wondering what's going to happen next, because something is unexpected and different.

So what is the best way to practise in order to achieve the quickest progress? I have another story. A professional classical guitarist, George, contacted me several years ago with a challenge. He had heard about our swim coaching and the unique way we taught, and he was inspired to try and create his own method of teaching classical guitar as a result, using a similar philosophy. He was a non-swimmer. He had no trauma based around being in water or swimming, which is important to this story, but he could not swim. His challenge to me was for us to work together for five months, at the end of which he would expect to swim really well. He agreed to be a model student; his words were, "I am at your mercy, and I will follow everything you instruct me to do to the letter, including video documentation and blog posts about my practice between sessions." I accepted the challenge. Now, it's fair to say that he was already at an advantage because of his profession. He had a 'deliberate practice' mindset that made him the incredible classical guitarist that he is, having spent many, many hours on repetitive cords and exercises over the years. We began our first lesson with a video analysis, which allowed me to start teaching him about the process and how swimming works. In that first lesson, we managed to get him connected and balanced in the water, his feet slightly came off the bottom of the pool for a moment, and he was then able to do about four or five strokes in this position. True to his word, he went away and practised exactly as I asked him, starting with one thought process or cue at a time, doing short repeats of the drill and then putting this thought process into his whole stroke swimming, all without taking a breath to begin with. He would then repeat this process with the next cue. We followed this regime over the next four months. We had nine lessons in total, and at the end of this period, he was swimming as well as any of the coaches that I worked with. As the months passed, we simply incrementally increased the difficulty of both the stroke thought processes and, more importantly, his focus. We started by thinking of just one thing at a time, and then as his nervous system was adapting to the new skills, we were able to put thought processes together in a process called chunking. Each time we introduced a new skill, he would think about this new skill in isolation to begin with. Then we would slowly start to build a sequence of skills that blend together in fluid movement patterns, just like a movie where single pictures are built to create an animated whole. You will see example swim sessions in Appendix 1 following this method, blending skills that we refer to as A, B, and C.

Spiral learning

What is spiral learning? And why is it the foundational ideal behind SwimMastery?

Spiral learning is a teaching method based on the idea that a student can learn more about a subject each time it is reviewed or revisited. Each time a student encounters the topic, there is an opportunity for their knowledge, understanding and skill level to improve.

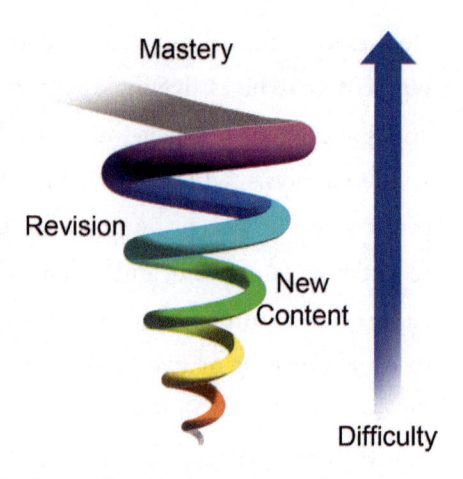

When a swimmer first embarks on their journey to skill mastery, they have very little understanding, proprioception and related body awareness and therefore, their ability to focus or interpret the instructions is greatly reduced. This makes it imperative that the prompts that are given or used are matched to the swimmer's current level of competence in these three areas (knowledge, understanding and skill level). In this book, we use the word 'cue' to refer to a specific instruction for each new movement pattern or process. The level of focus and attention needed to apply each cue is achievable by the swimmer at their current level, who can, therefore, interpret the prompt. After some focused and mindful practice, this pattern or process will become automated, both as a movement and as a neural pathway, and will have greatly increased the swimmer's body awareness whilst, of course, imprinting a new default swimming movement.

With this increased awareness and understanding, the swimmer will be able to revisit the same topics at a higher level when the cues and thought patterns become more targeted and intricate.

I talk to my students about spiral learning when they first start their coaching journey with me, asking them to imagine that when they walked through the door, they stepped onto the bottom rung of their own personal spiral staircase leading towards swimming mastery. I explain to them that on that lowest rung of the spiral staircase, they have the proprioception, body position and awareness, and consequent feel for the water that they walked in with. The journey is all about using swimming movement patterns to improve in all of these areas, so as we make our way up the spiral staircase and to the higher rungs, with better understanding, they are able to revisit swimming movement patterns with improved proprioception, body awareness, and control. In the beginning, we use less detail and easier thought processes, and then, as proprioception and body awareness increase, we are able to go into more detail and more intricate thought processes. This enables us to continually improve.

We are seeking progress, not perfection. The reality is that I can never tick a box as 'perfect' with any element of my stroke. For example, I will never have perfected my head position, rotation, or arm recovery because I can always approach a skill from a higher level of knowledge and understanding. This spiral learning is as important to me in my coaching skills as it is in my own swimming; in both areas, I aim to continue on the upward spiral forever. I will never know everything about coaching, the body, the strokes, or the brain. Therefore, as my awareness in each of these areas develops, so do my opportunities for learning.

A swimmer stays in this spiral cycle for as long as they want to achieve mastery. You choose your desired level of mastery, and you decide when or if you have achieved it. This will link closely with your goals. You might find that you adjust or revise your current goal as you progress towards it or achieve it. Warning! This striving for mastery in your skill can become addictive. One client came to me with an initial goal to take part in a Sprint Triathlon (400m) and got so absorbed in the process of improving his stroke that, a few years into his journey, he swam the length of Lake Windermere (18.6km). Congratulations Yasu Kimura!

To Focus or Not Focus? That is the question

Swimmers often tell me about how they love to go for a swim to switch off and not think about anything. My question back to them is, "Are you really switching off? Or, are you actually thinking about what emails you have to write or what you are going to have for lunch?"

Is it possible to not think?

Is it actually possible to not think about anything? For those of you who practise meditation, what would your answer be? I often hear people telling me that they can't meditate because they can't stop thinking. Are they setting themselves up to fail, I wonder? I suggest that, for the next two minutes, just close your eyes take a moment away from the book, and think of nothing …. How did that go? Even if you were thinking about thinking of nothing, you are technically still thinking of something because you are thinking of thinking about nothing – confusing, right? The reality is that there will always be thoughts in our minds. Meditation, for example, is simply the ability to notice those thoughts and let them go or, in some forms of meditation, it is about focusing on a specific word or mantra to help you stay 'in the moment'.

If we can't *stop* thinking, we can choose *what* we think about. As we discussed previously, until a new movement pattern is automated, we need to be disciplined in our attention to the specifics of the pattern. Remember that we cannot focus on more than one new thing at a time, so our time in the pool is best spent attending to improving our swimming by focusing on particular elements of it.

Don't think of a pink elephant!

My guess is that you are currently doing just that! When I ask a swimmer what they were thinking about during the last swim, they often give me a list of things they were trying not to do. For example, they were focussing on not lifting their head or not over-rotating. However, the mere fact that their focus was on over-rotating - or not - for instance, probably led to them over-rotating because this was the dominant concept in their brain.

The only way to make the positive improvement we want is to make that concept dominant in the brain. *You cannot do a don't - you can only do a do!*

Attention to detail

The idea is to focus on one thing at a time to begin with. For example, send your head away from your feet, firstly taking six non-breathing strokes and then adding in some breathing strokes while maintaining the focus on sending your head away from your feet. The key to success when you are focusing on sending your head away from your feet is to not worry about any other elements of the stroke that may be going wrong during that repeat. It is very common for a swimmer to set off with one cue in mind and then spend the rest of the repeat noticing and berating themselves about the other things that are not going well. For example, my head is in the wrong place, my legs are too low, et cetera. The very fact that you are noticing these things tells you that you are actually no longer focused on the cue you set off with. Practising in this way is a soul-destroying journey, as the focus is continually on what's going wrong rather than on making a specific change in that moment. It is common for these things to pop into your head as you are going down the pool, and the skill is to return to and maintain your focus on your chosen cue.

When working with swimmers, my primary task is to help them improve their ability to focus on making the changes we are addressing in their technique. In our busy worlds, focus doesn't come easily; people's minds are always racing with all the things they have to do and the places they have to be. It takes a lot of concentration and practice to quieten the mind enough to focus on the technique cues at hand. One very useful tool that I encourage my swimmers to use is the attention to detail score (ATD). The swimmer marks their attention, i.e. their ability to actually focus on the cue they have set off with, out of ten, with one being not focused at all and ten being completely focused. This serves two purposes: to hold the swimmer accountable for their focus and to give the swimmer a measure of their focus. The instruction I give is for the swimmer to aim to improve their attention to detail score on every single repeat. The objective over a series of sessions is to improve the average attention to detail score for each specific cue.

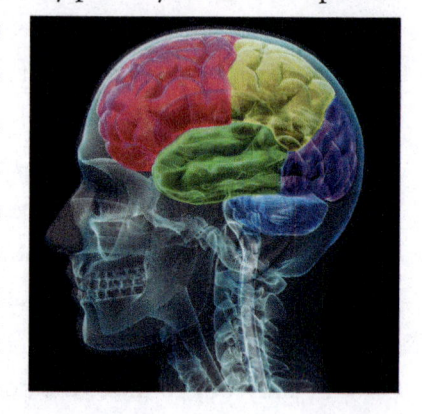

Blending of cues

Once you feel confident that you are consistently able to achieve the position or movement pattern that a particular cue is aiming for, begin to blend cues to create whole, more fluid movements.

I always recommend taking 3 cues to the pool for a session. Let us call these A, B and C. In this example:

- A send your head away from your feet
- B rotate the whole body
- C direct energy forwards through your middle trident prong

Begin with 4 repeats of cue A, then B, then C. Then start blending cues A and B together and give this blend of cues an attention-to-detail (ATD) score for 4 repeats. Continue with A + C and B + C. Eventually, you are aiming to be able to blend the 3 cues A + B + C. As your skill increases, you will be able to blend more cues, resulting in a fluid perpetual forward movement.

Make the most of your learning preferences

Identifying your own preferred learning style will help you to choose the right cue to accelerate your learning. A useful approach to thinking about learning styles describes three types of learners: visual, auditory and kinaesthetic.

Visual learners, as the name suggests, learn best by observing. Video feedback is particularly powerful for visual learners. Watching demonstrations performed by your coach will have a far greater impact if you are a visual learner than listening to their instruction. You will also find pictures and diagrams very useful—for example, SwimMastery's *Illustrated Guide to Freestyle*. Visualisation is an excellent technique for any visual learner, and usually, the more absurd the visualisation, the easier it is to imprint. For example, rotate your whole body, from your shoulders down to your feet. Imagine your whole body is a remote control. A remote control is solid and cannot bend or twist. So simply imagine rotating your remote control down the pool.

Examples of cues for a visual learner:
- Imagine your body, from your shoulders to your feet, is a remote control
- Imagine you are sending energy forward through three prongs of a trident

Auditory learners learn best by listening to or hearing an instruction. If you are an auditory learner, you may also benefit from noticing the sounds you make whilst swimming, and using this as your feedback loop. For example, one excellent cue is to swim quietly and tune into any sound you are making as you swim; this is a great way of testing whether you were able to achieve that or not.

Examples of cues for an audible learner
- Make a small pop pop popping sound as you exhale out through the nose.
- Rotate silently to streamline

Kinaesthetic learners are doers and feelers. They learn by doing and experiencing. You will be able to identify yourself as a kinaesthetic learner if you often use statements such as, "I feel this… …". Tactile feedback from a coach is particularly helpful if you are a kinaesthetic learner. Another great feedback loop for a kinaesthetic learner is to tune into the sensations you feel on your body and within your body. For example, how the water pressure feels against different body parts, or what the pelvis feels like when it is in the correct position.

Examples of cues for a kinaesthetic learner
- Feel the water supporting your face as you rest it in the water.
- Feel the water pressure on the front of your fingernails as you extend into your *Streamline* position.

When coaching, I always tune in to the language that a swimmer uses so I can identify, as quickly as possible, what style of learner they are, and then use the appropriate cues to support this, particularly at the beginning of their swimming journey. However, I also encourage the use of cues from the other two learning styles to create a more solid and rounded learning experience. To find your preferred learning style, it is important to try out cues based on each of the styles and see which ones you respond to best, both in terms of how easily you are able to focus on the cue and how it feels in the stroke. Bear in mind, though, that sometimes working with a new cue may feel strange. This is more likely to be because it is different to what you are used to feeling rather than because you are not doing it right.

A Consistent Push-off

Why practise your push-off?

In this section, we are talking about a standard push-off the wall of a pool that one would use at the start of each repeat when practising swimming. It differs from a competitive 'break-out'.

You are using the push-off to give you a stable platform to begin working on your stroke. Therefore, how you push off from the wall must aid the set-up of the position you need for freestyle. Many swimmers push-off with one arm out in front and begin stroking immediately. Some even add a breath into that first stroke directly off the wall, which they definitely don't need as they have just had the opportunity to breathe at the wall. Pushing off in this way means the body is disconnected before you even begin your practice. As you will learn in the next few chapters, connecting parts of the body together is key to swimming effectively and ensuring we are tapping into larger muscle systems. Therefore, we recommend having both arms out in front of your head in the correct position before pushing off from the wall. (the Build The Frame with Arms position you will learn about in Chapter 4).

You can use the momentum gained from pushing off the wall to begin your first strokes, benefiting from the sensations and the body position that this momentum will give you. This allows you an opportunity to feel what a balanced body position is. When we have experienced that sensation, we are more likely to recreate it than if we had never felt the sensation. Many open-water swimmers tell me that they do not see the benefit of learning an effective push-off in the pool since they are only ever going to swim in open water where there are no walls. That may be so; however, there are many benefits to technique improvement that can be obtained through an effective push-off when practising in a swimming pool.

A consistent push-off during your swim practice in a pool is also paramount to being able to use metrics effectively to help you accurately monitor any gain in speed, as discussed further in Chapter 13.

Pool Toys

You may own, or will certainly have seen, a pull buoy, hand paddles, and kickboard. These are very common pieces of equipment that many swimmers take to the pool. Their intended purpose is to aid and encourage an effective 'pull' or 'kick'. When you have started to put into practice some of the ideas we have talked about in the chapters on *Flutter* and *Catch*, it will hopefully become very obvious how these pool aids can actually do more harm than good. Regarding the catch, the shoulder joint is the most unstable joint in the human body, and therefore we must take extra measures to protect it and to ensure we are not putting the joint into a compromised position or putting too much load on it. Some other pool toys, that do not compromise the positions or movements of our joints, have more potential to help improve swimming skills and performance.

Pull buoy

This is a small, figure of eight-shaped, piece of foam that swimmers put between their thighs to give the legs extra buoyancy so they are not required to kick, that is, putting all the focus on the 'pull' element of the stroke. Firstly, as we will discover in the Chapter 5 on *Flutter*, we cannot swim efficiently without using our legs. Having this buoyancy aid between the thighs lifts the swimmer's legs to the surface and also serves to hinder the swimmer's ability to rotate using the whole body. This and the fact that the swimmer is not using their legs causes the swimmer's body to 'banana' and enhances the fishtailing of the back end, leaving the swimmer to rely solely on their arms to pull themselves along. This puts an enormous amount of load on the shoulder joint, and it also creates a completely disconnected stroke that is solely being driven by the pulling action. Practising this encourages a break in the connections and the all-important synchronisation points, where the magic actually happens. It also encourages the swimmer to focus on 'pulling' when what we actually need to focus on is a well-timed holding action or *Catch*.

Hand paddles

Hand paddles come in all shapes and sizes from big plate-sized pieces of plastic down to tiny finger paddles. No matter what the size they also have the same purpose, to focus on the pull. This focus brings many of the same outcomes on the swimmer's body and movement patterns as a pull buoy.

Often the reason why swimmers choose to use these aids is in order to strengthen and 'train' specific muscles. This would only benefit them if they are actually using the muscles they are intending to use, and this would only be possible with the correct movement patterns. Very few people are able to create correct movement patterns with these swim aids, even if they can without them, due to the added buoyancy or surface area they have.

Kickboard

Swimmers hold the board (usually at the back end) as they attempt to kick themselves up and down the length. Because of physics and anatomy, this poses a problem: the kickboard is typically made of foam or plastic and, therefore, floats at the surface of the water. This means that as the swimmer holds onto the board, their hands are always at the surface of the water. Having the hands in that position puts the arms too high and causes the scapulae (shoulder blades) to depress and retract, i.e. to move towards the spine and away from your ears. As a consequence of that scapula position, the ribcage will posteriorly tilt, and the pelvis will anteriorly tilt, causing the lower back to arch excessively and the hip flexors to shorten. All of this leads the swimmer to perform a kicking motion much like that of kicking a football, driven almost solely by the quads and hamstrings and causing the feet to kick up and down from the knee. So, the very tool (or toy, as we like to call them) that they are using to help them kick is actually hindering them by causing an incorrect body position and, therefore, an inability to move the legs using the correct position and muscles.

To move our legs without compromising the connections needed for a streamlined, efficient body position, the pelvis must be slightly posteriorly tilted, with only a moderate arch in the lower back, and elongated hip flexors. In this position, where we also access muscles in the core, including the abs, glutes, spinal stabilisers, and obliques, movement of the legs flows from the hips. In contrast, a kick from the knee driven by the quads and hamstrings is very inefficient because these are large muscles and very oxygen hungry, so it can cause the swimmer to tire easily. Furthermore, this kicking motion creates an excessive amount of form drag, as the bend in the knee breaks the *Streamline* position and puts the brakes on. It also creates wave drag: through the knee bend, the foot tends to break the surface of the water and create splash and lots of bubbles behind the swimmer, which can slow them down. You will find out more about this in Chapters 4 and 5 on *Building the Frame* and *Flutter*.

Tempo Trainer™

The Finis Tempo Trainer™ is a metronome that helps you consistently hold a chosen stroke rate. It is a fantastic way to create measurable improvements, working with stroke count. To swim faster, use Mode 1: speed up the tempo (reduce the seconds per stroke) while maintaining the same stroke count per length; alternatively, maintain the same tempo while reducing your stroke count.

Snorkel

A front-mounted snorkel is an excellent pool toy to use when you are in a busy pool that doesn't allow you to stand up to reoxygenate and refocus. It allows you to swim whole lengths, staying with the cue and not needing to turn the head, disrupting your body position and attention, to breathe. I recommend purchasing the longer version, which works best for the head position that is essential for a well-connected body position and, eventually, for getting a well-integrated breath into your stroke without interrupting your forward momentum. I would suggest only ever using the snorkel for half of each practice session, so it does not become a crutch or an obstacle to learning your breath management skills and integrated breathing techniques.

Session Planning

It is very easy to turn up at your local pool intending to swim but without having any idea of the skills you are going to work on during that session. A lot of swimmers jump in the pool, start swimming, and then begin what I call 'enquiry'. They spend a few lengths scanning their body, the feel of the water, perhaps counting their strokes, to find all the things that may be wrong with their stroke, and then begin the arduous task of attempting to correct each and every one of these during that swim. This results in a very unfocussed and discombobulated session. Instead of this unhelpful, reactive way of spending your time in the pool we recommend a proactive approach, actively planning each session before you leave for the pool.

We provide some example session plans and practice sets in Appendix 1. You will see that each set has example cues labelled A, B and C. For each repeat, there is space for you to log your Attention to Detail Score. As you work through this book you can reuse the sets by substituting the cues. Your attention to detail score will be your measure of when you are ready to increase the repeat distance, as this is first and foremost about evolving and improving your technique. If your attention to detail scores are consistently low or decreasing during a swim session, either change your cues, and see if your scores improve, or change to a different stroke for a few lengths (if you swim other strokes), then come back to the set and your attention may improve. Or sometimes it is best, at this point, to end the session and try again another day when you are feeling more able to focus.

We recommend that you use these plans as they are. As your technical skill and/or conditioning improves you can increase the difficulty by gradually increasing the distance of repeats within the sets. Sticking to the plan will help keep you focussed and minimise the possibility of you undoing what you have achieved by spending time during your session 'just swimming. It is best to get out of the pool having just swum your best and most focussed length.

Chapter 3

Air Exchange

We need air for survival. It keeps us alive, and we have inbuilt reflexes to ensure that the constant breathing cycle is never interrupted, even when sleeping. However, swimming presents an obvious obstacle to breathing naturally.

Spending some time considering breathing, and by that, I mean the actual air exchange in the lungs, is of utmost importance and can make all the difference in swimming. I have often come across clients who have a high level of cardiovascular fitness but who are not able to complete two lengths of a 25m pool without becoming completely breathless. This is, typically, solely down to poor air exchange whilst swimming.

In day-to-day life, we ideally want to be breathing diaphragmatically, in through the nose and out through the nose. A lot of the population breathes in a dysfunctional way in their day-to-day lives, for example, not breathing diaphragmatically or not breathing both in and out through the nose while awake and asleep. Here, we will concentrate specifically on breathing in swimming.

Let's start with some exploration. Sit up nice and tall, imagining a piece of string pulling your head up towards the ceiling. Take a big deep breath in, either through your mouth or nose (for this exercise it doesn't matter which). What happens next? I expect that you instantly wanted to let out that air. How did you feel when you took the deep breath? What muscles did you feel engaging? Did your chest rise, and possibly your shoulders too? Did you suck your belly in towards the spine as your chest rose? Did it feel relaxing? Or did you feel some level of stress and anxiety that urged you to breathe out immediately? You may begin to see reasons why we don't ask swimmers to take a deep breath. Technically, we do want swimmers to take a deep breath, as we want the air to go deep into the lungs right down into the alveoli, which are the small air sacs in the lower lung. However, what we think is a deep breath is often, in fact, a big shallow breath, as you have probably just discovered. This is called paradoxical breathing.

Now take as much air, as big a breath as you can manage, into your lungs and notice how you feel and what you want to do next. There is a good chance that you experienced an immediate urge to exhale the air. And no doubt you felt quite tense and uncomfortable doing it. It is amazing how often I observe swimmers taking this type of breath each time they begin a length. This excessive in-breath immediately puts the body into a state of stress which the swimmer can find very challenging to recover from. As they have begun the length with an excessive in-breath, a cycle of heavy breathing begins, with excessive in-breaths and excessive out-breaths, resulting in the swimmer being breathless within one or two lengths because essentially they are hyperventilating. They then need to stop, recover for a few seconds or even minutes and then they begin the process again.

Sit up straight once more, take in another breath and this time draw the air down into the diaphragm, down past your belly button, and notice the difference in sensation in your body. Firstly, you should notice that the belly button moves outwards away from the spine as the air goes in. Secondly, you should notice much less movement in the upper chest and shoulder area, resulting in a more relaxed feel to the in-breath. And thirdly, you shouldn't have that huge desire to breathe out immediately.

The human brain has an inbuilt instinct that triggers inhalation after we have exhaled. As you sit reading this book, breathe out all the air you have in your lungs and see what happens next. No doubt (hopefully!), you inhaled automatically. When we think about swimming in relation to this reflex response to emptying the lungs, we can instantly see why swimmers tend to hold their breath when their face is submerged. Instinctively, the brain triggers inhalation once a person reaches a certain level of air hunger. When swimming, the brain is also fully aware that the face is submerged in water, and therefore, it does not want the body to breathe in because it is trying to protect itself from drowning. To deal with this paradox, the unaware swimmer will tend to breath-hold while the face is submerged. Note that when swimming, we are not looking to completely empty the lungs, or to fill the lungs maximally: this exercise is for demonstration purposes only.

To change the automatic response, you first need to draw your attention to it. Once you are aware of this automatic sequence taking place, you can begin to make changes to it. I would suggest swimming a few laps, observing what you do with your air exchange, and asking yourself the following questions:

- Are you taking an excessively deep breath before immersing your face?
- Can you feel where the air is going during that inhalation? Is it going into the upper chest cavity, or are you using the diaphragm to draw the air deeper into the lower part of your lungs?
- What do you do after you immerse your face? Do you hold on to the air until the last moment before the next inhalation? Do you explosively exhale as soon as your head enters the water? Or do you release the air gradually?

- Tune in to the actual air exchange process and ask yourself how you feel. Do you feel breathless? And if so, how soon into your swim do you begin to experience breathlessness?
- Tune in to how the muscles feel around your thoracic spine area: do they feel tense or relaxed?

All these observations will give you clear and useful information on your current air exchange practice. They will also give you a baseline for comparative measures as you introduce new practices and notice changes.

Diaphragmatic inhalation

What do we mean by diaphragmatic breathing? If you look at the human body and a picture showing the lungs (Figure 3.1), you will see that they take up a lot of space in the torso. The diaphragm is the biggest breathing muscle, and if we are breathing correctly then we should be predominantly relying on this muscle to breathe. The diaphragm sits at the base of the lungs and will contract and move downwards when a person inhales; then when the person exhales the diaphragm will relax and move upwards. Far too often we observe people not taking advantage of this muscle to breathe, resulting in shallow breaths that are mostly controlled by muscles in the upper chest. If you consciously engage the

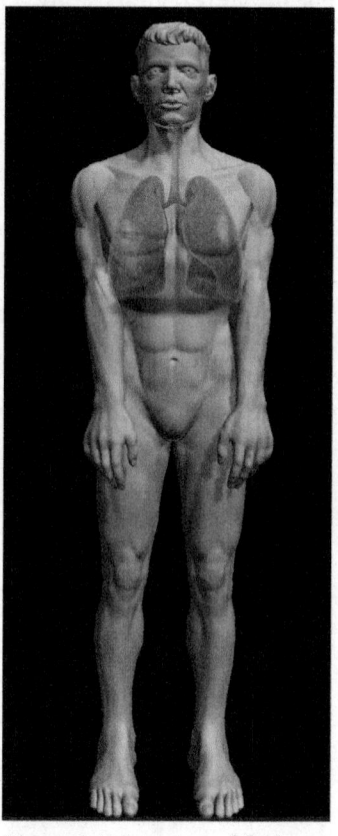

Figure 3.1: Location of the lungs

diaphragm, you will ensure full breaths that reach the lower regions of the lungs, and a more effective gaseous exchange at the alveoli. It is easy to tell if you are taking a truly diaphragmatic breath or not, by observing the movement of your abdomen during inhalation and exhalation. People often believe that good posture requires continuously held abdominal muscles. However, this can lead to rigidity that stops us from accessing correct breath mechanics rather than allowing our diaphragm to work as designed. It is important to note that at no point are we looking to completely empty or completely refill the lungs during the exhalation and inhalation; this could result in hyperventilation and tension in the body as a result.

The air exchange process plays two parts in swimming. Firstly, and most importantly, it is about survival, and oxygenating the blood, and it is also responsible for moisture and heat conservation. Secondly, it helps the swimmer to find balance by shifting the centre of mass. Sending air into the upper chest cavity will increase instability as the buoyancy will be too far forward, and, therefore, the centre of mass will not be optimal. By taking a diaphragmatic breath, we are able to send the air lower down the body, changing the buoyancy point and allowing the swimmer to achieve better balance because the centre of mass is in a more optimal position, as discussed in Chapter 1. (See Figure 3.2).

The first step to improving the air exchange process is focusing on the in-breath. When a human breathes through their mouth, it will typically be more of a thoracic (chest) breath, using many smaller muscles and resulting in a less satisfying shallow breath. Breathing in through the nose will typically be more of a diaphragmatic breath. However, during swimming, it is not possible to breathe in through the nose as there is too great a risk of inhaling water directly into the lungs and choking. Therefore, the breath must be taken in through the mouth, and as it is not natural for a mouth breath to be a diaphragmatic breath, we have to learn how to do this and practise it as much as possible.

The SwimMastery Way

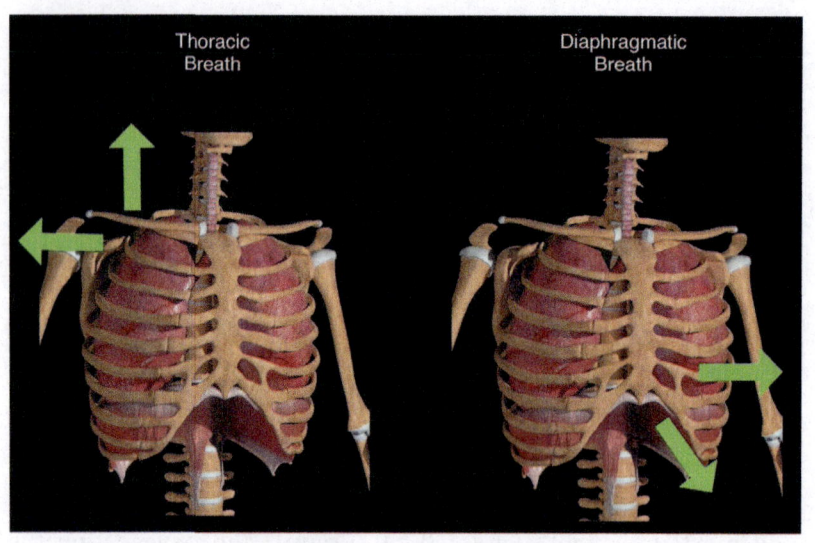

Figure 3.2: Where do we send the air?

Dryland activity 3.1 Diaphragmatic breathing

Stand up nice and tall as if you are sending your head towards the ceiling, opening up the space between your diaphragm and your sternum.

If possible, stand in front of a mirror so you can see movement in the belly and chest area rather than just feeling it. Place one hand on your chest and the other hand over your belly button. Take as quiet a breath in through your mouth as possible.

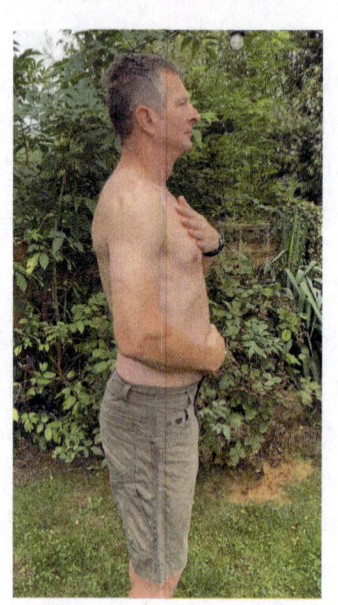

Figure 3.3: Thoracic breath

If you can hear the air going in, chances are this will be a thoracic breath and you will notice the top hand moving outwards and upwards. Breathe in silently through the mouth, sending the air down to the hand that is on your belly button and pushing it outwards towards the mirror. Yes, we have to let our waistlines go during this exercise; it is not possible to hold that stomach in, so just let it go!

Then, gently allow the air to escape through your nose. Repeat this until you can find a rhythm that feels comfortable and helps to maintain a feeling of relaxation. In through the mouth, push the hand over the belly button away from the spine, then slowly release the air through the nose, allowing the hand to return towards the spine. If you are doing this exercise in front of the mirror, observe which part of your body is moving during the inhalation and the exhalation. You should expect to see the belly and lower rib cage area expanding during the inhalation.

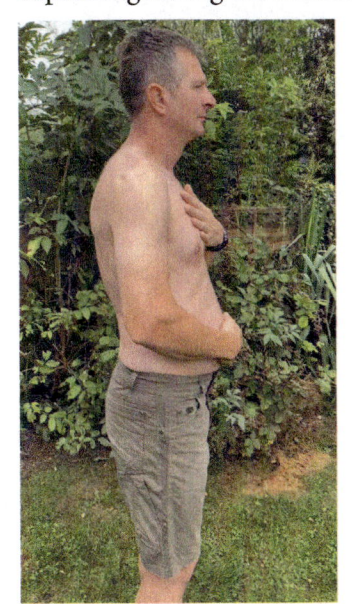

Figure 3.4: Diaphragmatic breath

Keep the chest and shoulders still; if they are expanding or indeed lifting, then your breath is too big and too shallow.

Once the above exercise feels relatively easy to achieve, you can concentrate more on the exhalation through your nose. Take your diaphragmatic belly breath in, inflating the belly and sending the hand outwards away from the spine, and then allow the air out through your nose during

The SwimMastery Way

the exhalation. How long can you make that exhalation last whilst remaining comfortable and relaxed? You want to exhale slowly in a controlled way for as long as possible, but not to the point of severe air hunger. Once you have finished your long, controlled exhalation, you should easily be able to take another controlled breath in quietly, using the diaphragm.

Pool Activity 3.1 Diaphragmatic breathing

» Put one hand on your belly and one hand on your chest.
» Inhale through your mouth. The hand on your belly moves out, away from your spine.
» Exhale through your nose with a slow release of air.
» The hand on your belly moves inwards towards your spine.
» The hand on your chest stays still throughout.

Figure 3.5: Diaphragmatic breathing practice, standing in the pool.

Nose breathing

There is no evidence showing any benefit of mouth breathing. Breathing through the mouth will sometimes occur when the sympathetic nervous system is activated as a fear response (when a person is in fight, flight or freeze mode) or when we have severe air hunger through excessive exercise. However, many people worldwide have dysfunctional breathing habits and are predominantly mouth breathers. This presents an added challenge for swimmers, who should breathe out through the nose. As we have spoken about before, swimming itself can be a sympathetic nervous system activator due to the mere fact that we cannot survive in water.

The nose is designed explicitly as the breathing organ. In addition to the gaseous exchange advantages of breathing using the nose, there is also a psychological benefit. Nose breathing, especially during exhalation, stimulates the vagus nerve, which activates the parasympathetic nervous system. This has a substantial calming effect, helping to keep the swimmer relaxed. To enhance the stimulation of the vagus nerve, you can hum during the steady, continuous exhale.

The nose also plays a role in hydration management and temperature control. You can lose up to 30% more moisture and heat by exhaling through the mouth instead of the nose. Some animals, including dogs and horses, use this heat loss by panting significantly when their core temperature rises. Conserving body heat becomes a critical factor if you want to swim in excessively cold water or cold water over a very long distance, such as the English Channel. Hypothermia and dehydration are two of the most significant contributors to swimmers failing this kind of challenge, so if we can regulate our exhalation to minimise the heat and moisture loss and maintain better oxygenation in the blood, it is worth doing.

During rest intervals, when you begin swimming sets, we recommend nose breathing. This will reduce your recovery time between repeats.

Pool activity 3.2 Buoyancy Test

Now you have spent some time working on the inhalation and the exhalation, let's take it to the pool. Start with a buoyancy test.

Figure 3.6: Buoyancy test holding the breath – (a) floating with toes on the floor, and (b) floating in a ball.

Take a breath in and submerge yourself in the water in a floating position, holding your breath. Allow your toes to rest on the floor of the pool if need be. Relax as much as you can and just feel the sensation of your body floating and take note of your position in the water. Where can you feel the surface of the water on your body? Make a mental note, then stand up.

You could also do this by curling up into a ball and making the same observations.

Take another breath in and submerge yourself again, but this time expel all your air very quickly to the point where your lungs are empty and observe what happens to your body. Did it stay in the same place as in the previous exercise? Where do you feel the surface of the water now on your body?

Figure 3.7: Buoyancy test expelling all the air – (a) floating with toes on the floor, and (b) floating in a ball.

Figure 3.8: Buoyancy test slowly releasing the air – (a) floating with toes on the floor, and (b) floating in a ball.

Most probably you are lower in the water than you were in the previous exercise. Make a mental note, then stand up.

Now take a diaphragmatic breath as you have recently practised. It is helpful to start by having your hand on your belly button to give you physical feedback. Then submerge and allow the air to slowly release from your nose with a steady stream of little bubbles. Stay as relaxed as you can, ensuring that the exhalation is continuous, controlled and leaves you feeling completely relaxed.

What happens to your body during this exercise? Notice your position in the water. Notice where you feel the surface of the water on your body. What happens as you continue to exhale: do you stay in one place, or do you eventually start to sink? Make a mental note then stand up.

Once you have done this exercise correctly, which could be after a few practices, you will notice that your body position in the water is similar to its position during the first exercise.

Pool activity 3.3 Exhalation

Once you become more familiar with the steady exhalation in Pool activity 3.2, it is then an interesting practice to time the duration of your exhalation, remembering that it is a continuous, controlled stream of bubbles out through your nose. This should feel relaxed as if you could carry on doing it all day. If you are feeling uncomfortable or stressed as if you are holding your breath, just increase the number of bubbles you are releasing, keeping them small and controlled until you feel relaxed. Again this will take practice, but persevere to find your correct exhalation. Make a note of the time you achieve and see if you can improve on this during your swimming journey. It is common to be able to release bubbles in this way for over 40 seconds.

Dryland activity 3.2 Exhalation at home

You can carry out a variation of the above pool exercises in your own home in a washing-up bowl at the kitchen table. For those who find this difficult or perhaps have phobias or anxiety around water, this is probably a better way to start, as you will have only your face in the water. You will know that you have found the correct amount of inhalation and exhalation when you can continue the exercise without stopping for more than 2 to 3 minutes. With your hands on the table on each side of the bowl, bend your elbows to lower your face to just above the water, diaphragmatic inhale, submerge, and exhale your steady stream of bubbles for as long as possible, remembering you are not going to the point of complete air hunger, then straighten your arms to lift your face from the water, take another relaxed diaphragmatic inhale and repeat, keeping the cycle going for two to three minutes without stopping.

> ### Pool activity 3.4 Short repeat whole stroke swimming
>
> Practise your new air exchange skills in your swimming, focusing only on the in-breath and the out-breath. Bend your knees to lower your body into the water, then with one hand on your belly button take a diaphragmatic breath in, tip your head into the water and then push off. As soon as your face is submerged begin your slow trickle of bubbles; continue this while swimming 6 to 8 slow relaxed strokes. Then stand up and repeat. You should also breathe this way when practising any of the drills in this book. What is important when working on air exchange is that you give it its own focus. Many swimmers are guilty of not allowing themselves to focus purely on the air exchange and therefore they never successfully imprint the new skills into their swimming.

Exhaling in whole stroke swimming

Up to now, you have only practised the first two steps of the three steps you need for air exchange in swimming. We have concentrated on the inhalation and the first part of the exhalation, which is the exhalation that can be used during drill practice or short repeat whole stroke swimming practice. Both of these types of practice can last anything from 5 to 15 seconds. However, during whole stroke swimming, we typically have to complete our air exchange cycle in two or three seconds depending on whether we are taking a breath every two or every three strokes. If you just stuck with exhaling as you did in Pool activity 3.4, you would very quickly become breathless because you would be holding on to too much air, leaving no room for the next inhalation. We need to bring in the final step to expel enough air for this shallow breathing not to happen.

The SwimMastery Way

The exercise below can be practised in the pool or in a bowl of water at home.

> ### Pool activity 3.5 Air exchange in 3 steps
>
> Take a quiet, relaxed diaphragmatic breath in, submerge, begin your steady stream of bubbles out through your nose for two seconds and then, as if you are snorting or imagining that you are using your nose to clear away the water around it, perform a quick sharp exhalation through the nose. The timing of this sharp exhale is timed with the moment that you have started rotating to air to take the breath in, so that it is complete at the moment your mouth clears the water, allowing you to simply take or allow your next diaphragmatic, relaxed, controlled in-breath through your mouth (See Figure 3.9).
>
> **Figure 3.9:** Air exchange – (a) Step 1: Steady bubbles with head in neutral, (b) Step 2: Sharp exhalation, and (c) Step 3: Allow inbreath.
>
> Keep repeating this exercise until you feel comfortable doing it continuously for more than five minutes. It should be

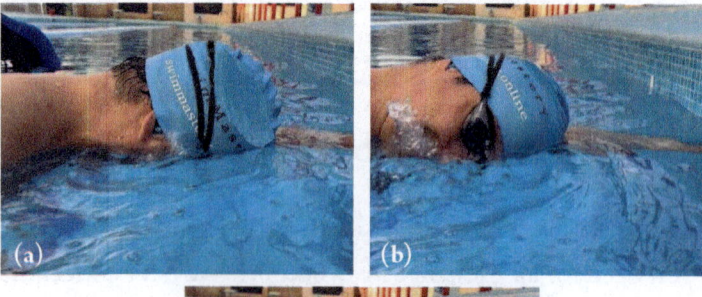

continuous but relaxed, making you feel as if you could survive breathing that way forever, should you need to. If you are not feeling relaxed and you are getting breathless, then make some changes until you feel relaxed.

Notice the following to identify adjustments that you may need on the in-breath:

» Is it diaphragmatic?
» Are you inhaling too much or too little?

And on the out-breath:

» Are there bubbles when you first submerge your head?
» Are the bubbles, when you first submerge your head, too big?
» Are you beginning the explosive exhalation too early, which could result in an increased feeling of air hunger which will put the body under stress?

Try adjusting these one at a time until you feel completely relaxed, and can do it continuously for five minutes without stopping.

How often should you breathe?

This is a very common discussion between swimmers and swim coaches. And there are many schools of thought around the world. Should I breathe every two, three, or four strokes, or even every five or six?

To be honest there isn't a definitive answer to this question, as it is dependent on so many factors. For example: tempo of the stroke, distance to be covered during the swim, lung capacity, and breathing health of the swimmer, to name a few.

The question I always ask my swimmers when we discuss this topic is, how often do they breathe whilst running or cycling, or during other land-based physical exercises? This is usually met with a puzzled look as of course they very seldom even think about when to breathe whilst running or cycling. They don't breathe on a certain number of strides or a certain number of turns of the pedal; more often than not they breathe when they need to. Why? Because they can. As we spoke about in Chapter One, there is one obvious obstacle to breathing when we want whilst swimming, which is that our faces are submerged in water. But if we take the question of how often you breathe when running and cycling into account, with the answer being when you need to, then surely the same should apply to swimming? Our muscles are dependent on oxygenated blood to feed them and to keep them moving, and therefore it is imperative that we do not interrupt this cycle, especially on longer swims. In the Olympics or World Championships, we now see most swimmers (of course, there are always a few exceptions to every rule) predominantly breathing every two strokes for distances greater than 100 m. If the Olympians are doing this, in my opinion, we should too.

Having said that though, and as mentioned previously, there are factors that can change this. Often people talk about bilateral breathing. Whenever anybody mentions bilateral breathing to me, my first question to them is 'What does bilateral breathing mean to you?' And almost without fail the answer I get to this question is 'I must breathe every three strokes.' But is that the correct definition of bilateral breathing? No. Bilateral breathing simply means taking an equal number of breaths on each side. So we could encourage swimmers to breathe 20 strokes to the right and then 20 strokes to the left and they would still be breathing bilaterally. Bilateral breathing is very important for anybody wanting to swim efficient freestyle, as one-sided breathing can cause a multitude of compensations and imbalances.

Hypoxic training

There is a place in the swimming world for hypoxic training. However, in my opinion, too many swimmers are practising hypoxic training without learning how to do it safely. There is a lot more to hypoxic training than simply breathing every five, seven or nine strokes. With the correct instruction and guidance, swimming is an effective tool for improving the ability to tolerate carbon dioxide and can hugely improve a swimmer's daily breathing health. But my recommendation if you want to undertake this is that you do so with a qualified Oxygen Advantage® Instructor.

"So how often should I breathe?" I hear you still asking. My generic answer is to encourage all swimmers (with the exception of sprint races where they breathe very little) to breathe every 2nd stroke whilst ensuring that they are practising equally on both sides i.e. every 2nd stroke to the left for one length and every 2nd stroke to the right for the next length and so on. However, it can be beneficial to breathe less whilst focusing on technique and swimming very short distances, for example in 25m repeats which give you the opportunity to recover your breathing before beginning the next length.

'Sinkers'

When working with a swimmer who has labelled themselves a sinker, the first thing that I will work on will be air management, as this is often the cause of the sinking. As I explain in more detail in the next chapter, incorrect air management will lead to an activation of the sympathetic nervous system, inducing a stress response and increased tension in the body. And we know tensed muscles are denser than relaxed muscles. The more dense something is, the more likely it is to sink. For example, driftwood is very porous and floats, whereas lead is very dense and sinks like a stone. The other contributing factor regarding air management is which part of the thoracic cavity we are breathing into. If we are drawing air primarily into the upper thoracic cavity, our balloon/buoyancy aid is higher up in the body, leaving the denser muscle and bone with no help from the increased buoyancy that more air in the lower thoracic cavity could provide with diaphragmatic breathing.

Once I have worked on air management I will sometimes ask the swimmer to hold their breath after taking a diaphragmatic inhalation, and then lie in the water so the extra buoyancy can help them to feel that support. It is sometimes just a matter of the body feeling that the water will support it once or twice, for the person to relax and allow it to happen. I practise this several times with them and will then ask them to once again float but this time to bubble out slowly through their nose and notice how their buoyancy doesn't really change very much even though they are exhaling albeit gently. I will then ask them to try floating once again but this time explosively exhaling as much air as they can and ask them to notice what happens to their bodies. This will cause the body to begin to sink, some more than others. And I finish off by once again asking them to bubble out slowly so they can feel the difference and learn to surrender to and trust the support of the water. A phrase I often use whilst coaching is, 'The water will do the work if you allow it to, but it will fight back if you fight it.'

Air exchange: Summary of cues

» Steady exhalation through nose
» Sharp exhalation through nose
» Diaphragmatic inhalation through mouth

If you are interested in further exploring your day to day breathing functionality in more depth, we recommend contacting an Oxygen Advantage® instructor.

Chapter 4

Building the frame

As discussed in Chapter 1, our human bodies get in the way when we swim. If we look at all aquatic mammals and the shapes of their bodies and their body makeup, we will notice that they have far fewer moving parts than we do. A dolphin, for instance, doesn't have any. Its body is flexible but doesn't have the capability of hinging, so in effect, it is born with the frame that we are going to talk about, already in place.

We are built with the ability to move our extremities and other parts of our bodies at will. Of course, when you look at yourself in the mirror, it is easy to see where these movements take place; it is probably not something you have thought about, as it is just being a land animal. However, when we swim, these moving parts must become the centre of our focus during the foundational learning sessions, whether by self-coaching or working with a SwimMastery coach.

Connection: torso to leg

The first step is to make the human body more like that of an aquatic mammal. The hinge that causes the most significant problem whilst swimming freestyle and backstroke is the hip joint. Humans can literally bend themselves in half. It is easy for our hips to remain straight when we are standing, with gravity working vertically through our joints. However, when lying horizontally in the water, the effects of gravity make this much more difficult. Legs are made up of bone and muscle and are incredibly heavy. If we are bent at the hips, our legs sink and cause an enormous amount of drag. Traditionally, swimmers feel they only have one option to combat sinking legs, and that is to kick the legs as fast and as hard as possible to keep them at the surface. Often, this is subconscious. It does indeed work, giving the swimmer a sense of 'false' balance, but the payoff is too great regarding energy cost and forward momentum. The effort required to achieve this is enormous, as we are trying to defy the laws of gravity. Connecting the legs to the torso, in the same way we naturally do when standing, creates a unified frame from shoulders to feet, making it possible to shift weight and find 'true' balance.

This connection will be the first in a long line of connections we are going to discuss throughout this book. To connect the legs to the torso, we must get in touch with our true core. As you started reading this paragraph, the moment I mentioned the word 'core', did you instantly think about your abdominal muscles? This is often the case: when I ask my clients where their core is, they point to their stomachs. My next question is, when you eat an apple, are you left with the core only on one side? The quizzical looks that then ensue are amusing but serve the purpose of inviting the client to think a little more deeply about what the word 'core' actually means in their own bodies.

Now begin the investigation into your own body and discover, firstly, what it is that you *do* feel when engaging your core, and secondly, what it is that we *should* feel with core engagement.

Dryland activity 4.1: Connecting legs to torso

Stand up with your legs within your hips, so your feet are no wider than hip distance apart and your legs are not squeezed together. Imagine you are trying to touch the ceiling or sky

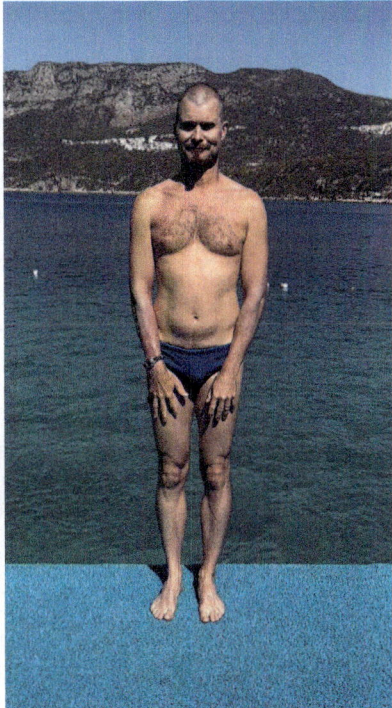

Figure 4.1: Standing tall.

with the top of your head, assuming it is in a neutral position as it would be when standing and looking straight forward. You are not trying to touch the ceiling or sky with your forehead. Or you could imagine you have a book on top of your head. You are looking for the book to be stable, i.e., not slip off frontwards or backwards; this will only be possible with a neutral head position. Lightly rest the inside of both elbows along the front of the ribcage, allowing the lower arms to hang down in a relaxed position.

Take a moment to ensure that your neck is relaxed and neutral as you try to touch the ceiling or sky with the top of your head, and just feel what happens in your body. Which muscles do you feel engaging as you make yourself taller? It is almost as if you're trying to get air in between each of your vertebrae, and between each of your lower ribs. Then slouch down again, and once again stand up tall: what engages? Make a mental note of it. Common answers include: my abdominal muscles, shoulder muscles, and sometimes the glutes.

Now stand in the same position, imagining that you are touching the ceiling with the top of your head. Place the inside of your elbow onto the front of the ribcage allowing the rest of the lower arm and hand to relax and hang down. This keeps your frame compact and also ensures that the arms are moulded to the body and out of the way during the Build The Frame without Arms drill (see Pool Activity 4.2.1 below). Note, the arms and shoulders should feel relaxed in this position. A common error that swimmers make is to hunch the shoulders and press the arms into the body or towards the legs, each of which will disconnect the frame we are trying to build.

Now take a moment to check your pelvis position. Place your finger and thumb on the top of your iliac crest (hip bones) at the front and the back on each side. Gently, and with very small movements, tilt your pelvis anteriorly (the forefinger goes down), and then posteriorly (the forefinger goes up). See figures 4.2a and 4.2b. You want these movements to be very slow and very small, causing no discomfort and absolutely no pain. If there is discomfort or pain please stop immediately or reduce the amount of movement to ease the discomfort. At this stage, you're just looking for movement. As you tilt your pelvis anteriorly and posteriorly, imagine it as a swinging pendulum: move between the two end ranges without pausing, with your thumb and forefinger moving down and up. Be sure to maintain imaginary contact with

Building the frame

Figure 4.2: (a) Tilting your pelvis anteriorly and (b) tilting your pelvis posteriorly.

your head on the ceiling or sky during this practice, to ensure that you are in fact only tilting your pelvis, and not bending your whole torso backwards and forwards. If, when you are posteriorly tilting, your knees begin to bend or buckle, you have gone too far. Remember these movements are very small, so moving slowly is essential to allow you to tune in and feel different muscles engaging.

Have you found some movement in the pelvis? To reiterate, it does not need to be a big movement; it may even be just a few millimetres. Now make contact with the ceiling or sky once more, and get in touch with the muscles that you felt engaging at the beginning of this exercise. Whilst maintaining this position now slightly tilt the pelvis posteriorly and tune in to the muscles you feel engaging. Has anything changed?

Have you lost any of the sensations you had at the beginning? Or have those muscles remained engaged, and more muscles have now joined in? If the answer is yes to the last question, make a note of which muscles have now engaged.

To sum up, to find the position that you need to maintain when swimming freestyle, tilt posteriorly, very slowly, and aim to stop at the point where you feel the most muscle engagement. Be sure to keep your tall posture as you find this point. See Figure 4.3.

Figure 4.3: Correct swim posture.

Now you've found your torso to leg connection, by tilting your pelvis, let's talk about the core in the human body in more detail.

How shall we think about the core in order to use it to improve our swimming? The core is the midsection of the body, including the front, back and sides. It is all the way around just like the trunk of a tree. Muscles in this section of the body work as stabilisers for the entire body. We use these muscles all day every day when standing, sitting, walking and of course in every sport. In Dryland Activity 4.1 we are looking to engage muscles including abdominals, obliques and spinal erectors. We will also connect further down the body through the glutes and the hip flexors.

- Hip flexors
- Obliques
- Abdominals

- Spinal erectors
- Obliques
- Glutes

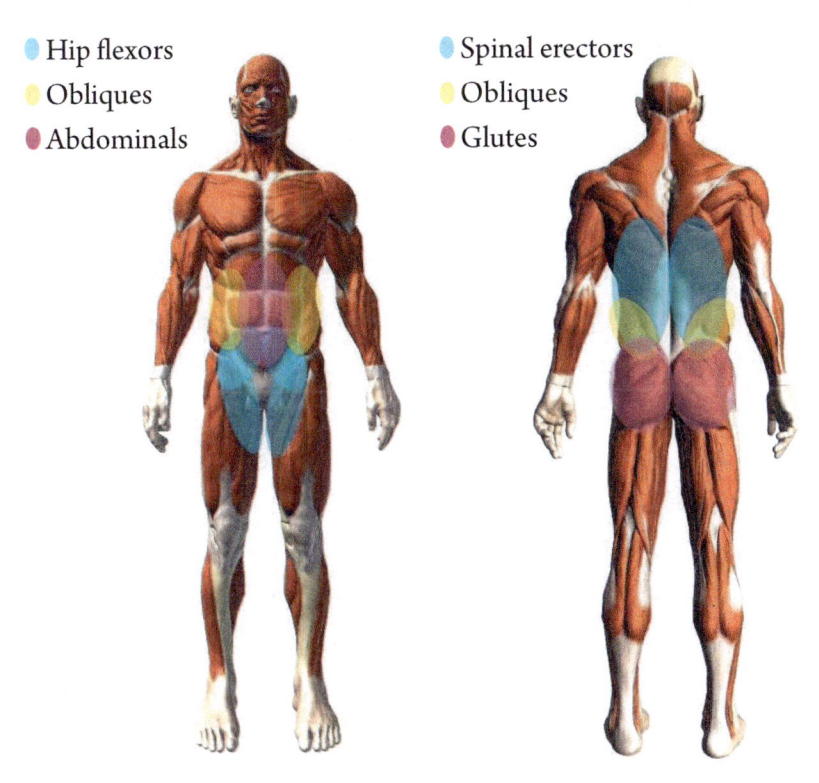

Figure 4.4: Connecting legs to torso: muscles.

You may have had the abdominal muscles and possibly the glutes on your first list. I trust that, once you had moved your pelvis, you felt some muscles in the spine and even your hip flexors. Through experience, I have found that swimmers rarely consider the hip flexors and certainly rarely feel them. But once you have some length in that area it is much easier to maintain that position horizontally which is, of course, our ultimate goal.

It may appear counter-intuitive, but this standing exercise is the best way to start practising your swimming, and I suggest that my clients do it as often as possible in front of the mirror so they can see how their body reacts to the movements they are performing. As you use this book, your mirror will become your best friend. Proprioception is one of our biggest challenges (see Chapter 1), and therefore having that feedback from your mirror is invaluable.

Connection: torso head

Now let's address your head position. Talking about the head position is actually really simple, as it is simply neutral. However, maintaining this position when horizontal and face down in a medium you cannot survive in, it becomes less simple. We have an automatic need to be able to see the air that we breathe (see Chapter 1), therefore instinctively we have the urge to lift our head when horizontal in water.

Finding your correct head position in water is potentially very straightforward because you simply allow the water to find it for you. Turning off all the muscles in the back of your neck allows your head to float in the correct position: neutral. However, even though it should be very easy to find the head position in freestyle, we frequently sit at desks or use devices for hours at a time, so our neck muscles are incredibly difficult to turn off.

As you sit reading this book, I would like you to look to your left, now look to your right, now look up at the ceiling, now look at the floor. And ask yourself one question, What were you using to follow these instructions? Yes, your neck muscles. The very muscles we want to turn off when swimming.

This shows how, if you follow a cue for where to look while swimming, your head position will be incorrect by the pure nature of performing the action. Of course, achieving a neutral head position is easier said than done. As mentioned above, many of us spend a lot of time with our heads in an incorrect position looking at devices and working on computers, and as a result many of us are very tense in the neck and upper shoulder regions making it very difficult to then switch off these muscles whilst immersed in water. Sixteen years after first thinking about this, I am still working on it in my own swimming.

> ### Pool activity 4.1 Head
>
> It takes a little practice to fight the urge to lift our head, and I suggest doing it by floating on your front. Simply allow every single muscle in your body to switch off, and feel what happens. Your torso will float; for this exercise it is immaterial whether your legs float or not. Now that you trust that your torso will float, do it once again and notice what happens to your head when you truly turn off all the muscles in the back of your neck. Yes, it floats too! Next time someone calls you airhead, say "Thank you, because that helps me with my swimming".
>
> **Figure 4.5:** Floating head.

Connection: scapula (shoulder blade)

Lastly, let's add your arms to the frame. From now on, when I refer to arms I would like you to imagine they are simply extensions of your scapula. This helps us to connect the arms to the frame that we have already started to create. We want our limbs to function as part of the whole body and never separately. As soon as we separate out any limb movement we instantly run the increased risk of injury and an inefficient stroke.

Dryland activity 4.2 Scapula slide

First, you need to become aware of your scapulae and how they feel in your aligned position. Stand up against the wall with the back of your head touching the wall, the back of your scapulae touching the wall, and your buttocks touching the wall. You will have your heels one to two inches away from the wall so you can maintain alignment. Imagine taking your head up towards the ceiling or sky, feeling your core muscles engaging. Once you feel aligned just notice for a moment what parts of your head, scapulae and buttocks are making contact with the wall. This alignment is the same as the horizontal alignment you are looking for in the water. If any of these three points of contact are missing, this provides you with useful feedback

Figure 4.6: Making contact with the wall.

about the challenges you face in achieving the body position you need in the water.

Now stretch both arms up as high as you can as if you are trying to touch your fingers to the ceiling above your head. As you do this, notice what changes in your alignment, particularly in the skull, the rib cage, and the pelvis. You should feel changes in the sensation of these body parts against the wall. Did you notice your scapulae slide down the wall, your buttocks slide slightly up the wall, and your lower back

Building the frame

come away from the wall, creating an arch? Take a moment to feel all the tension that this position is causing. You are probably feeling a lot of tension in your traps, your lats and probably even in your abdominal muscles and lower back. You probably now have more lordosis – the inward curve of the lower spine associated with anterior tilt in the pelvis. This will disengage all the muscles you previously worked to engage.

Relax and shake your arms out, and once again raise your arms up all the way to the ceiling to the same uncomfortable feeling you had before, and then very slowly bring your arms forward. You will probably only move the arms a few centimetres before feeling all the tension disappear. The moment you feel the traps relax, see if you can slide the bottom of your scapulae upwards, sending your cuticles towards the ceiling. You should feel that you have a

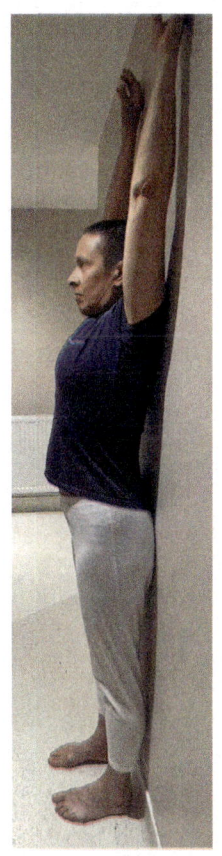

Figure 4.7: Tension and disconnection.

- Traps
- Lats

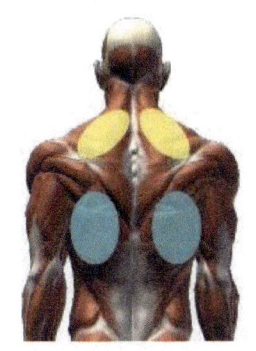

Figure 4.8: Scapula slide: muscles.

The SwimMastery Way

nice amount of movement in your scapulae. We're talking a few centimetres, definitely not 'stretching'. It's a gentle, easy, relaxed slide. Your body alignment should now feel as close to the starting position above as possible. With your arms in the correct position you should feel your scapulae flatten against the wall, your buttocks slide down slightly and your lower back flattens towards the wall easing all of the tension. This will be a familiar feeling from when you were posteriorly tilting your pelvis while standing tall.

From this position once again stretch your arms to the ceiling and then slowly move them forwards, noticing how your buttocks, scapulae and head position move against the wall, taking you out of alignment, and then back into it. Moving in both of these directions provides a feedback loop to build your body awareness.

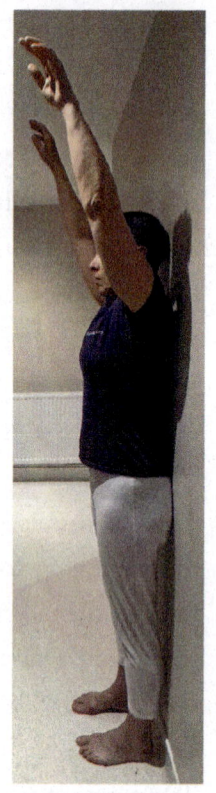

Figure 4.9: Sliding your scapulae.

Now step away from the wall and get into your best Build the Frame position, with three points of contact against an imaginary wall. In this standing position, lift both your arms and imagine your arms being an extension of your scapulae. Now use your scapulae to send your cuticles to the ceiling. Notice how you can move your arms towards the ceiling and back down again with your sliding scapulae.

A way to check that you are doing this correctly is to repeat this exercise but stretching your arms too high and keeping them there, and then see what happens when you try to slide the scapulae. You will probably find that the scapulae do not move freely as they are locked. And if you take the arms too low and try to slide the scapulae, you will see that your cuticles will move forwards instead of upwards towards the ceiling.

Figure 4.10: Scapulae send cuticles to the ceiling/sky.

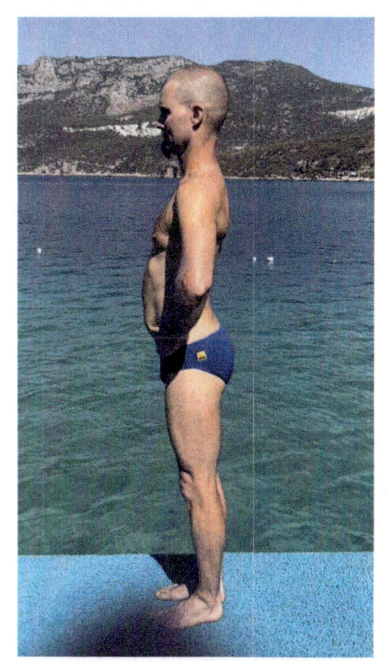

Figure 4.11: Scapulae cannot move freely – (a) Arms too low and (b) arms too high.

Once you have established the correct position, including the posteriorly tilted pelvis in Dryland activity 4.1, when you add in the arms you should be able to maintain the core engagement that you felt earlier. There should be no discomfort. It is very beneficial to practise these positions whilst out of the water so you become familiar with the movements that lead to the required muscle engagement. Then when you get into the water it is just a matter of being able to transfer that vertical body position and muscle engagement to the horizontal swimming position.

This connected body position is one that you need to maintain throughout each stroke cycle, albeit you are of course going to add in whole-body rotation.

Connection between pelvis and ribcage

When anteriorly and posteriorly tilting your pelvis, you may have begun to notice that your ribcage was also moving. When you tilt your pelvis, you are automatically extending or flexing your lumbar (lower) spine, which affects the extension or flexion of the thoracic (upper) spine, resulting in movement of the ribcage. When you are anteriorly tilting your pelvis, this should result in a posteriorly tilting ribcage, causing a bigger curve (lordosis) in the lower back. When you are posteriorly tilting your pelvis, this should result in an anteriorly tilting ribcage, and create less of a curve in your lower back. And the reverse is true: tilting the ribcage should lead to the opposing tilt in the pelvis.

The ribcage, along with the spine and the arm, drive the direction that the scapula moves in. The scapula is a highly complex bone structure which is often referred to as a floating bone as it floats over the ribcage, attached to the skeleton via 17 muscles. This gives an indication of how very complex the movement of the scapula is, with its many different and often contradictory directional terms.

Therefore, we have chosen to simplify how we describe the movement of the scapula by merely referring to it as being upwards and downwards movement when vertical doing standing rehearsals, and forwards and backwards movement when horizontal.

Loss of connection between pelvis and ribcage

When working on whole-body alignment in the water in a horizontal position, it is interesting to note the effect of one part of the body being out of alignment with the rest of the body. For example, if a swimmer lifts their head and looks forwards, that will cause the scapulae to slide backwards and cause a posterior tilt of the ribcage. This will create an increased extension in the lumbar spine, causing a bigger curve in the lower back, and the swimmer will often excessively anteriorly tilt the pelvis in an unconscious attempt to counter this and keep the legs at the surface. This then creates a shortening of the hip flexors and makes it impossible for their legs to remain connected to the torso, which often causes the legs to drop or splay. Similarly, if the legs, by dropping, are the first part of the body to lose alignment, the swimmer will often extend the lumbar spine in an attempt to raise the lower end of the body, triggering the same shortening of the hip flexors and loss of connection between the legs and torso. Pressing the head down into the water is as unhelpful as lifting the head up: this also leads to the legs dropping and the same compensations as above.

The human body is connected through 360 joints, and a loss of connection in one part will always have a knock-on effect elsewhere. Learning to connect our body parts in the correct way is vital to enable us to maintain alignment down the body throughout the entire stroke cycle.

In the water

Once you feel you can access these positions on land by practising the exercises above, your body should be able to find the same, or similar, sensations in the water.

A note on drills and immediate whole stroke practice

The important thing to remember about drills in the water is that they are just a snapshot in time. We are looking to help our body feel a specific position just for a moment and not to move down the pool, so try not to pay attention to how far you are travelling as it is not important, it is about what you are feeling. We want to use the drills to teach our bodies the sensation, and then take that sensation straight into our whole stroke. Initially, I would recommend you practise the whole stroke without taking a breath while you imprint the new sensation, as taking a breath will interrupt this.

I recommend having three cues per drill, for example, send your head away from your feet, feel long, and tilt the pelvis. Take your first cue and repeat the drill three or four times, standing up between repeats. Next, push off with the same cue or thought you chose to use in the drill and do 4 to 6 whole freestyle strokes with that same thought. At this stage, because you are now more aware of what you should and shouldn't be doing, it is tempting to berate yourself for everything else that isn't going right. It takes practice and discipline to let those negative feelings go and bring your focus back to the particular cue you are working on. Learning to stick to the actual cue is surprisingly challenging but it will be your key to success. Once you've been through this cycle with your first cue, then repeat it using each of the other two. So just to reiterate, for each cue you will do 3 to 4 repeats of the drill and then a series of 4 to 6 whole strokes of freestyle maintaining the focus on the chosen cue.

Building the frame

Next, choose the first cue, push off and go straight into whole stroke. I would recommend that the first six strokes of the length are non-breathing strokes, to give your brain a chance to focus on the sensation it is looking for, then add in breathing for the rest of the length, trying to maintain focus on the cue rather than focussing on the breath.

The process of learning to swim is about being able to integrate into your freestyle the sensations you feel whilst doing the standing rehearsal and the water-based drill. Practising instant integration is crucial to achieving this. If you rush through the drills, switch between cues too quickly, or don't immediately integrate them into whole stroke, your nervous system will not remember the sensations and your practice will not have the desired effect.

Pool activity 4.2 Connections

4.2.1 Connection: torso to leg

Figure 4.12: Arms moulded to your body.

I recommend practising the standing rehearsal in the water just before beginning the drill, to remind your body of the sensations it feels in that particular position. Imagine you are touching the ceiling with the top of your head, making yourself feel tall, and with air in between each one of your vertebrae. Put your pelvis into the position that allows you to feel some length in the hip flexor area, and some glute engagement.

Now, lower yourself into the water by bending your knees, and pushing yourself very lightly off the floor, sending your head away from your feet. Imagine your feet are being left behind on the back wall of the pool, so you can feel that same sensation you just felt standing up. In this first drill, your arms should be moulded to your body as in figure 4.12 with your forearms just inside your front hip bones. If you find you are having to consciously adjust the pelvis in your standing rehearsal, then on your next repeat make this the cue you focus on once you have pushed off. Cues:

» Send your head away from your feet
» Tilt pelvis posteriorly

4.2.2 Connection: head

Repeat the process with the head connection. Choose three cues to focus on, i.e.

» Relax the muscles in the back of your neck
» Allow the water to support your head
» Send your head away from your feet

Figure 4.13: Head connection.

When first introducing this new head position I would recommend doing Build the Frame with no arms, as in 4.2.1, but once it feels more natural you can also think about the head in Build the Frame with Arms, as in 4.2.3, and later on in the streamline drill too (See Chapter 6).

Until this connection has become automatic, you may find it helps to bend your knees and lower your shoulders fully into the water with the top of your head to the ceiling, then tip your head into the water before your gentle push-off.

4.2.3 Connection: scapula

Figure 4.14: Scapula connection in Build the Frame with arms.

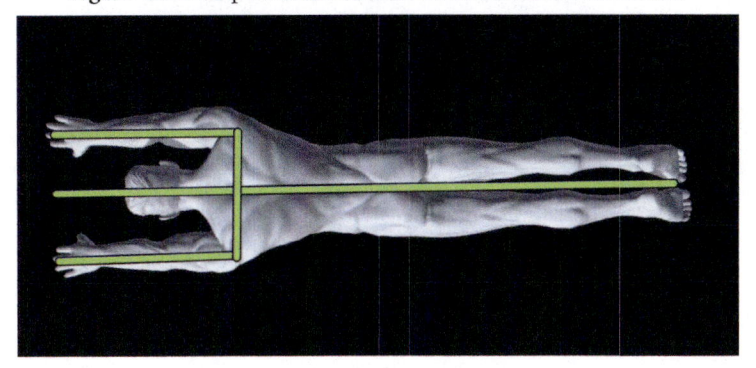

Figure 4.15: Trident.

Again I recommend practising the standing rehearsal that has hopefully, by now, become very familiar, to remind your body of the sensation it is aiming for. We are looking for the arms to be an extension of the scapulae: as you push off the floor imagine you are sliding your scapulae towards the wall of the pool in front of you. If your arms are connected to your scapulae, and your scapulae are in the right position, your body should feel somewhat lighter, and your legs may be slightly closer to the surface of the water.

Imagine your body as a trident (see Figure 4.15). The middle prong of your trident is your head, which you have sent away from your feet. The left and right prongs of the trident are extensions of the scapulae and end at the cuticles.

Practise these three cues:

» Slide your now elongated scapulae (including your arms) forwards
» Imagine your scapulae are sending your cuticles to the wall of the pool in front of you
» Imagine you are lengthening through all three prongs of the trident.

Using these cues, you will repeat the drill cycle described above for 3 to 4 repetitions each, then take what you have learned directly into whole stroke practice without breathing, then with breathing.

Building the Frame: Summary of cues

- » Send your head away from your feet.
- » Tilt pelvis posteriorly.
- » Relax the muscles in the back of your neck.
- » Allow the water to support your head.
- » Lengthen through your middle trident prong.
- » Slide your elongated scapulae forwards.
- » Imagine you are touching your cuticles to the other end of the pool.
- » Feel long through your head to your feet.
- » Imagine you are lengthening through all three prongs of the trident.

Chapter 5

Flutter

The legs are always an interesting subject when it comes to freestyle swimming, and there are many schools of thought out there. Triathlon coaches say don't use your legs at all, in an attempt to save the legs for the bike and the run. Traditional swimming coaching puts boards in swimmers' hands and asks them to kick-kick-kick-kick-kick to make as much splash as they possibly can – the bigger the splash, the better the kick. Some talk about a six-beat kick, while others talk about a two-beat kick or even a one beat kick.

I say, let's remove the word "kick" from our freestyle swimming vocabulary. As humans we have associations connected to words that are well-known, and kick is one of those words. Generally, if a person is asked to kick something, they will typically pull the foot back by bending at the knee, engaging the quadriceps muscles (quads) and hamstrings (see Figures 5.1 and 5.2), and firing those muscles to accelerate the lower leg through to make contact with the ball or the object that they are trying to kick, and then through the force of the kick the leg will ricochet back to its neutral position. This is a well-ingrained response to the word 'kick'. So, by removing this word we remove the temptation to automatically perform the wrong movement, which gives us an opportunity to rewire the nervous system.

The SwimMastery Way

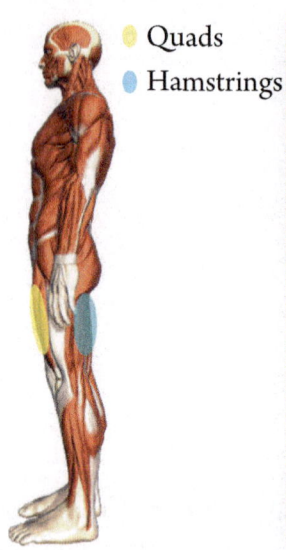

- Quads
- Hamstrings

Figure 5.1: Muscles engaged to 'kick'connection.

Figure 5.2: Kicking.

Now, the reality is that in order to swim freestyle efficiently, the legs must be involved. However, it is how we involve the legs that will determine if they are helping us or hindering us.

If the swimmer does not use their legs at all, this will result in the legs, which comprise a large proportion of the body mass, being disconnected and therefore not controlled, causing them to wave in a fishtail manner behind the torso and for some causing the fishtailing legs to sink. This causes a huge amount of drag, both laterally and vertically. Equally, if we do use the legs but kick them excessively, as hard and as fast as we can, they will again disconnect, and be difficult to control, and often the resistance created by all the bubbles and splash will be greater than the propulsive opportunity.

Let's talk more about a continuous flutter, or as it's known in the swimming world, a six-beat kick (three kicks per side). When we look at all the sprinters in elite swimming, we can see them doing a continuous kicking motion. More often than not, this is a six-beat kick.

In most pool facilities and leisure centres around the world, you will see kickboards lying around. Often, swimmers will hold a board and attempt to kick themselves up and down the length of the pool. Because of physics, this poses a problem: the kickboard is typically made of foam or plastic and therefore floats on the surface of the water. This means that in order for the swimmer to hold onto the board, their hands will always be at the surface of the water. Now we know from our *Build the Frame with Arms* section in Chapter 4, and the dryland and water-based practices, that having the hands in that position puts the arms too high and causes the scapulae to depress and retract i.e. slide backwards. As a consequence of that scapula position, the ribcage and the pelvis move into incorrect positions, causing the lower back to arch excessively, with an anterior tilt of the pelvis and a shortening of the hip flexors. All of this causes the swimmer to perform a kicking motion much like that of kicking a football, driven almost solely by the quads and hamstrings and causing the feet to kick up and down from the knee. So the very tool that they think is helping them is actually hindering them by causing an incorrect body position, and therefore an inability to perform the flutter motion using the correct position and muscles. Furthermore, a kick driven by the quads and hamstrings is very inefficient because these are large muscles and very oxygen hungry, so it can cause the swimmer to tire easily. This kicking motion from the knee also creates an excessive amount of drag: form drag because the bend in the knee breaks the *Streamline* position and puts the brakes on; and also wave drag because the knee bend causes the foot to rise towards or even break the surface of the water, and create splash and lots of bubbles behind the swimmer. Both types of drag can slow the swimmer down.

So how are the Olympians doing it? As we've already discussed, the sprinters are using a continuous flutter. If you study any of these elite swimmers under the water, you will see that when they are fluttering, it is not breaking their body line. They are continuously maintaining form whilst continuously moving their legs. None of them has an excessive knee bend, which shows they can't be relying on their quads and hamstrings. Yes, the knees do bend, but have you ever slowed down some underwater footage to see at which point their knee bends? We'll explore that more in Chapter 10.

So the question is, how can we use our legs effectively without compromising our non-negotiable frame? We need to do this by using muscle groups we began to access in our very first drill, the core: predominantly the abs, glutes, extensors, obliques, and hip flexors.

Dryland Activity 5.1 Standing rehearsal

5.1.1 Thigh backwards

You will need a small step for this practice. Stand sideways on the step with your right foot as close to the edge as you can get it, and your left leg hanging down beside it. (See Figure 5.3) Now check in with the cues you used during the Build the Frame dryland rehearsal. Imagine you are trying to touch the ceiling with the top of your head, making yourself tall, as if you have air between each of your vertebrae and lower ribs. Tilt your pelvis if necessary (this is person-specific) so that you can feel the same position and muscle engagement you felt during your Build the Frame rehearsal.

Figure 5.3: Check in on a step.

Once you have performed your check-in, draw the back of the left thigh backwards. (See Figure 5.4). Once you have drawn the left thigh back, hold it there for a moment and notice what you feel. Can you notice which muscles have engaged during this movement? If you're not sure, return the left leg to its

Figure 5.4: Draw the thigh backwards.

neutral position (simply hanging), and once again, draw your left thigh backwards, keeping your leg straight. To reiterate, at this point, you are not pulling the back of your heel back, but the back of your thigh. As you perform this action, you are looking to feel your glutes engaging and your hip flexors on that same side lengthening. I want you to think of this as if you are moving the thigh bone backwards rather than engaging muscles. Be very mindful that you are not instructing the glutes to pull the leg back, but drawing the thigh bone back and noticing which muscles engage.

Now do the same thing on the other side by turning around so your left foot is close to the edge of the step, and your right leg is able to just hang down loosely. Before you draw the right thigh back, check your Build the Frame cues to ensure you have the right body position before you begin, otherwise, you will not feel the correct sensation. Once you've practised this a few times on each leg, make a mental note of any differences in sensation you may or may not feel on your right side versus your left side.

The SwimMastery Way

5.1.2 Thigh forwards

Next, standing in the same position with your right foot on the edge of the step and the left leg hanging down loosely from your hip, draw the back of the left thigh backwards as before, but this time instead of returning your leg to neutral, swing it through as if sending the front of your thigh just in front of your body line. Then, repeat several times (see Figure 5.5). During both of these exercises, the lower leg is relaxed as if hanging off the knee. Do not lock the knee, as this will induce tension and the incorrect movement.

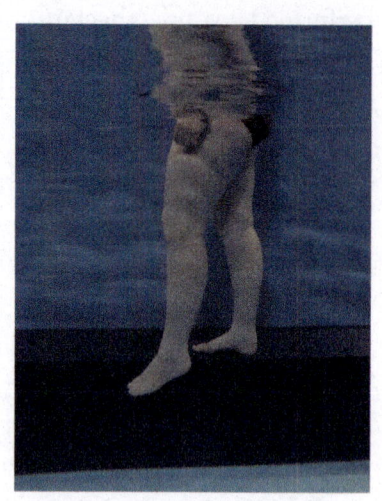

Figure 5.5: Swing the thigh forwards.

Pool activity 5.1

5.1.1 Thigh backwards and forwards

If you can find a step that you can stand on in the same way in the swimming pool, repeat these exercises the same way that you did them on dry land. The pressure of the water against the shin and front of the foot during this exercise gives you useful feedback, but it is not always possible to find such a step. Perhaps find a sinking toy, such as a brick that is often used for lifeguard training or children's lessons, and stand on that.

Figure 5.6: Swing the thigh backwards and forwards.

5.1.2 Ankles

When talking about legs, a common statement we often hear from swimmers is, 'I have stiff ankles'. Of course, true stiff ankles could make it more of a challenge without a doubt. However, most people who think they have stiff ankles, in fact, don't; they are simply holding tension in their ankles. A good way to test this is to stretch your leg out in front of you and just flex and point your foot (bend and stretch your ankle); if you have a fair range of movement when doing this, you don't have stiff ankles. If you do have stiff ankles there are several exercises you can do to help get more movement in this area.

Figure 5.7: Release muscles in your ankles.

> If you have some movement when pointing and flexing the foot, it could be a useful practice for you to perform the standing rehearsal in the water as in 5.1.1 above, focusing on moving the thigh backwards and forwards but feeling how the pressure of the water actually moves your foot for you. If your foot is not moving backwards and forwards then it is very likely that you are holding your foot in place. Take your attention to your ankle and try to actively release all the muscles, to allow the pressure of the water to move the foot backwards and forwards as you are performing the exercise above. Once you've released all the muscles in your ankles and your feet, repeat the standing rehearsal, and you should feel a completely different sensation when the foot responds to the water, remembering water is 800 times denser than air, and therefore provides a considerable amount of resistance if we let it.

Why are the legs important in swimming?

People often ask, "What are the legs for?" The most common answer amongst swimmers, and some coaches, around the world, is that the legs are there for balance. In truth, the legs are there for a type of balance, but the act of kicking the legs does not balance the body. Most swimmers think that they do balance the body, and therefore, they try and kick their legs as fast as they can to keep them up, and balanced. This results in the swimmer tiring very quickly in an effort to achieve something that can be achieved in a much smarter way by connecting the body and shifting weight.

What are the legs for then? They maintain rotation, act as an anchor, and are a counterbalance to the recovering arm on the other side. And of course, they do provide some forward propulsion if used correctly. The legs need to be in the correct position to provide this counterbalance rather than working hard and churning up water in an attempt to maintain balance. There is a difference. And changing how you think about the legs can instantly change how you use them.

It is impossible to swim efficiently without our legs being involved and engaged. To be able to begin to use your legs or improve your leg movement, you will first need to know or recognise what your current default leg movement is. Then you can move on from the rehearsals above to practising horizontally in the water. I give a couple of examples below: find the one that best matches your current default leg movement.

Pool activity 5.2

What do you currently do with your legs? Choose one of the following activities depending on what you tend to do more often.

5.2.1 Legs currently still

If you are currently not moving your legs whatsoever or indeed trying to keep them still, then your first task is to get the legs moving. I would recommend that you focus on the flutter, first following the dryland rehearsals above, and when possible, repeating the rehearsals in the swimming pool. Then introduce this movement to your *Build the Frame with Arms* position. When introducing the flutter to your *Build the Frame with Arms*, I find the cue that helps the most, to begin with, is to have a nice quick rhythm. If you try to move the legs too slowly in order to execute each movement correctly, you will find that you become disconnected and stiff, and the legs will feel very heavy and hard to control. We are looking for small, quick movements. When you are horizontal in your *Build the Frame with Arms* position, your focus changes from taking the back of the thigh backwards to taking the back of the thigh up towards the ceiling or the sky. We have an added benefit when we are horizontal because we can let gravity drop the leg for us. Therefore, you simply draw the back of the thigh up towards the ceiling and then repeat on the other side: lift-lift-lift-lift-lift in a very quick rhythm to begin with.

When you begin this exercise, it is very important that you are not trying to move down the pool. If you try to move forward, or to the other side of the pool, or have the intent of trying to be fast, you may start engaging your quads and hamstrings, and kicking your feet. In many cases, this makes a swimmer go backwards – the opposite of the desired outcome. Remember that at this point, you are introducing the leg movement to the *Build the Frame with Arms* position that you have already practised, therefore the alignment from your head to your feet is already in place, and the alignment between your rib cage and your pelvis is already set. When introducing the legs, you do not want to compromise either of these two positions.

Another excellent cue to think about when first introducing this movement is to imagine your thighs are paintbrushes, and you are trying to paint a small patch on the back wall of the pool directly behind the body. Usually, I ask my client to pick their favourite colour, and visualise this colour on the end of their brush, and then ask them to paint a small patch behind them, imagining that the back wall is a little too far away from them so they really have to make themselves long to be able to get the paint on the back wall. Note how I mentioned it is a very small patch, no bigger than the shadow of your body.

5.2.2 Legs currently kicking excessively

Over-kicking, or kicking too much, is often down to the fact that because we are not instinctually aquatic mammals, we attempt to use our limbs to keep our heads at the surface so that we can breathe. Over-kicking leads to two problems. Firstly, it is exhausting. When kicking excessively, you use smaller muscles and more power to attempt to keep the upper torso and head closer to the surface. When doing this, you are fighting against the water and not achieving much other than tiring yourself out. Secondly, over-kicking is predominantly driven by an excessive knee bend, which will cause an anteriorly tilted pelvis and a shortening of the hip flexors. This disconnects the legs from the torso, creates a huge amount of resistance, as we have spoken about previously, and means that the now disconnected body cannot move as one.

If you find yourself over-kicking, I recommend that you spend some time consciously quieting your legs. Swim whole stroke without taking a breath so that you can give all your focus to your quiet legs. Imagine that your feet are as far away from your head as you can; this will also help to quieten them down. Tune into the sound your legs make when you are swimming, as this is the best feedback loop for making these changes.

Repeat this focus several times until your brain can comprehend that kicking does not change your ability to stay balanced in the water. Our brains can talk us into doing things that are not necessary, simply because it doesn't understand the task at hand. And remember, as we are terrestrial mammals, our brains will be focused on land-based instincts that can work against us in water. Repeat this exercise, making the legs calmer and quieter with each repeat, until you feel that the legs are barely doing anything.

If you notice that you are still kicking from the knee and finding it difficult to move the whole leg, follow the steps above, starting with the standing rehearsals to build the new neurological pathways for a well-connected leg movement.

Two-beat kick

These days many swimmers are striving to learn a two-beat kick. However, whilst it can definitely be more efficient, if executed correctly, it is not a necessity. A well connected, well timed six-beat kick or flutter can be very effective and efficient too. The fact is that if you connect your legs and keep them behind the torso within the shadow of your body, then they are almost certainly going to be more efficient than before. With each year that goes by we are seeing more and more two-beat leg mechanics and variations thereof, in elite swimmers. However, a well-timed and connected two-beat leg movement can be very tricky, and therefore should not be attempted until you are absolutely certain that you have integrated the body connections covered in previous chapters. Over the years I have seen many swimmers who have attempted to teach themselves two-beat leg mechanics, often resulting in an excessive knee bend which has completely disconnected and interrupted their stroke. This has sometimes caused over-rotation and dead spots in the momentum that have then taken many months' practice, and sometimes longer, to correct.

So if we now know that the legs are not there purely for balance but as a counterbalance, do we need to be kicking all the time? The answer is, it's optional and very dependent on whether you are swimming a sprint, long-distance, or cross-channel event. Most importantly, it is dependent on the technique of the swimmer. Executing a flutter or a six-beat kick that is well-timed is definitely faster, there's no disputing this. However, it is not efficient over longer distances because the swimmer fatigues more quickly. Therefore, striving to learn a well-timed and connected two-beat leg movement will definitely be of benefit to those wanting to attempt the longer challenges. I will cover this in detail in Chapter 11.

Chapter 6

Streamline

This is probably one of my favourite subjects to speak about. I find it interesting to work out what the human body thinks is streamlined versus how the human body can actually be streamlined and still remain strong and avoid any chance of injury as it moves through the stroke.

What is streamline?

A dictionary definition of *Streamline* is:

"design or provide with a form that prevents very little resistance to a flow of air or water, increasing speed and ease of movement".

I have often had discussions about *Streamline* when working with swimmers over the years. I am always surprised to hear that they think that the more rotated they are in freestyle swimming (the more on the side they can get themselves), the more streamlined they will be. Although this would be true according to the first part of the dictionary definition, *a form that prevents little resistance to a flow of air or water*, it fails on the second part, which is *increasing in speed and ease of movement*.

What is the most streamlined position in freestyle? Let's explore different amounts of rotation and their effect on the body's mechanics and its ability to create and maintain forward momentum.

Let's begin by reminding ourselves of the 5% rule that we talked about in Chapter 1: when a human body is floating in water, 5% of the body mass will stay above the water, and 95% of the body mass will be submerged.

When the body is flat in the *Build the Frame with Arms* position, the back of the head, the top of the upper torso, and potentially the buttocks (depending on your centre of mass) will be above the surface (see Figure 6.1). The rest of the body will be submerged. Because there is so much surface area being presented by the body under the water, there is a huge amount of drag when moving forward. Through effective streamlining, while the 5% rule does not change, we can minimise this drag.

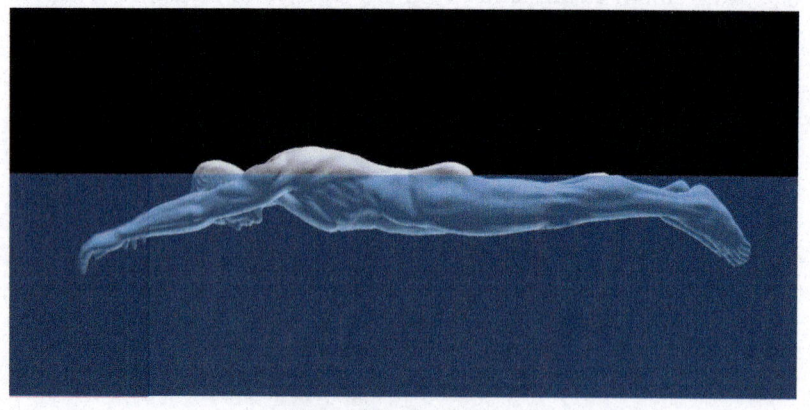

Figure 6.1: The 5% rule.

Dryland Activity 6.1 Find your rotated position

It is sometimes perceived that being completely on your side, at 90°, could be the most streamlined position in freestyle. Let's explore that.

Stand up, reach your right arm up to the ceiling and imagine that the wall on your right is the bottom of the pool (see Figure 6.2). With your arm in this position, look at that wall. How does it feel? Does your head feel comfortable? Can you actually see, or is your arm in the way? Are you having to distort your head position slightly, compromising the position of the arm, or rotate or twist your torso so that you can see the wall clearly?

Now walk up to the wall and stand side on to it in the position you've just practised, and put the pads of your fingers on the wall in that lengthened position and try to apply pressure. What does that feel like in your shoulder and scapula? How much strength do you feel you have in that position? Does it feel comfortable?

Figure 6.2: Reaching to the ceiling.

Now that you have explored the 90° position and discovered the discomfort and lack of strength available here, let's find a better position.

It is good practice to try this in front of a mirror to maintain eye contact with yourself; this keeps your head in place and allows you to see the body position you are creating.

Stand in your Build The Frame with Arms rehearsal position that we looked at in Chapter 4. Go through a mental checklist of all the cues you want to cover, finishing with ensuring that you are able to slide your scapula and cuticles to the ceiling.

Now imagine you have an arrow coming out of your belly button that is currently pointing straight towards the mirror or the wall in front of you (see Figure 6.4). Raise your heels to stand on the balls of your feet, and swivel your whole body, sending the arrow to the left corner of the room, ensuring you are still looking at yourself in the mirror or maintaining visual contact with the point you found on the wall in front of you (see Figure 6.3). This means that the head does not move; it stays in the same place. As you are swivelling your arrow to the left corner of the room, place your left arm along the front of your rib cage, with your forearm just inside your front hip bone. Once you have swivelled your arrow to the left corner of the room, return your heels to the ground and ensure that you centre your weight equally through each foot. When you are in this position, it is important that your whole body is rotated towards the corner of the room (see Figure 6.5).

Figure 6.3: Streamline rehearsal.

Figure 6.4: *Build the Frame with Arms* rehearsal.

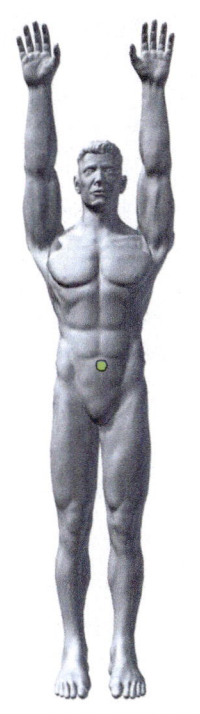

Figure 6.5: Streamline rehearsal with laser.

Imagine that you have eight laser beams coming out of your body, two coming out from your pecs, two coming out from your hipbones, two coming out from your knees, and two coming out from the front of your ankles. All eight laser beams should be pointing in the same direction. This is your Streamline standing rehearsal position. (see Figure 6.6). A common error during this standing rehearsal is to leave the feet behind and just swivel the body, causing a twist through the whole body.

Now return to your starting position, facing all laser beams forwards, head forwards and both scapulae, sending your fingernails to the ceiling, and repeat the same exercise, taking your arrow from your belly button to the right corner of the room whilst maintaining the head position. This time, your right arm will drop and lay along the front side of your rib cage, with your forearm just inside your front hip bone. Once again, put your heels down and ensure that you are centring your weight equally through both feet. Check that your whole body is pointing towards the corner of the room, apart from your head, which should still be looking straight forwards.

Figure 6.6: Streamline: 8 laser beams in the same direction.

Try it again on the first side. Go back to your Build the Frame with Arms standing rehearsal position, and go through your checklist. Then begin the movement again: take a small step forward with your right foot, slowly, allowing your left arm to drop down to your side. Allow the step forward to create the rotation in your body, and this time stop at the point it starts to feel uncomfortable and backtrack just enough to feel comfortable again. Once you reach the point that you feel is most comfortable, do another quick check-in with your Build the Frame cues, i.e. are you still able to touch the ceiling with the top of your head? Have you still put your pelvis into the correct position to feel length in the hip flexor area and glute engagement? And can you still slide the scapula and send the cuticles to the ceiling on the side where you have left the arm up?

> Practise this several times on both sides. Do you have different sensations when taking your right foot forward compared to taking your left foot forward? Once again, make a mental note or write down what you felt on a piece of paper. You're going to practise a similar exercise in the water, where you will be able to take the sensations you are feeling now in the dryland rehearsal but also feel the benefit of the actual weight shift created through gravity.

As you have already set the frame, every part of your body rotates at the same time and by the same amount, except for the head, which remains neutral. With the above dryland exercise, you will have been able to feel in your own body what the optimal amount of rotation should be.

If you were to lie on the floor in this position, your pec, your hip bone, and the front of your thigh would be making contact with the floor. We call these your 3 points of contact. In contrast, many swimmers think that it is the side of the body that should make contact with the floor. However, as you can see in Figure 6.7a this would clearly be over-rotated and would prevent you from having an aligned head. Figure 6.7b shows correct rotation and the resultant aligned head.

When we're thinking about *Streamline* we have to consider the need to present the smallest surface area when travelling forwards. But we also have to consider gravity, which is constantly forcing the body downwards.

Alongside managing the two laws of physics above, most importantly, we also have to consider the human body's safe and effective mechanics. And whilst we want to create the most streamlined position, we must at the same time ensure that we can still access our joints and levers in the safest and strongest way.

The SwimMastery Way

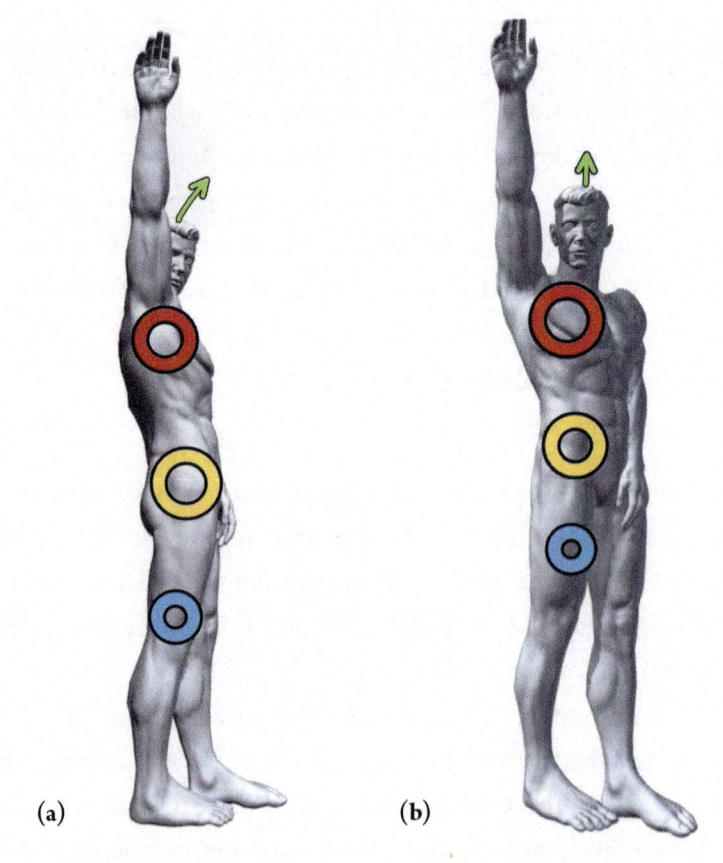

(a)   (b)

Figure 6.7: (a) Over-rotation showing 3 points of contact, and (b) correct rotation showing 3 points of contact.

This is not possible if the human body is completely on its side. As we have covered in Chapter 3, the most important aspect of learning to swim effectively and efficiently is to build the frame and then be able to maintain it during every movement of the stroke cycle. When we rotate fully onto one side, we can no longer do this.

You can see in Figure 6.8a over-rotation sending the streamline arm wide. In this position, the spine has extended, and the ribcage has moved with it. This locks the scapula in place, making it impossible for it to slide.

In Figure 6.8b, over-rotation is sending the streamline arm narrow. The spine has twisted in this position, causing the ribcage

Streamline

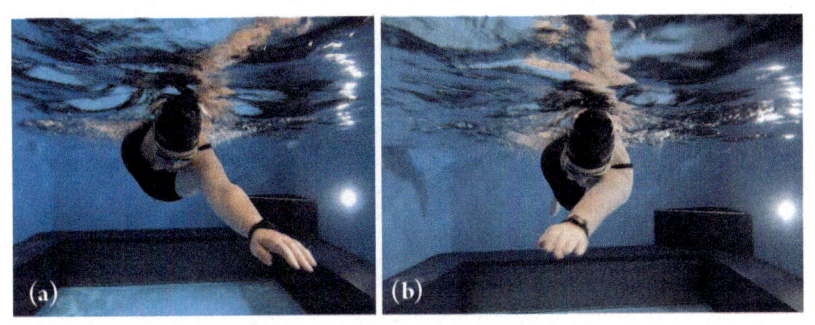

Figure 6.8: (a) Over-rotation with the streamline arm too wide, and (b) Over-rotation with the streamline arm too narrow.

to rotate further than the pelvis. The frame is, therefore, no longer in place.

The *Build the Frame* chapter has demonstrated that mobilising and sliding the scapula in the direction of travel is vital to connect the arm to the torso. We will explore the importance of this and the reason why an over-rotated position makes it impossible to perform the *Catch* in Chapter 9.

In freestyle, *Streamline* is the most important position to find. We need to dynamically move from *Streamline* on one side to *Streamline* on the other. This is made more difficult, and takes longer, when the body is over-rotated. Not only do we have to take into account the amount of time required to go from *Streamline* on one side to *Streamline* on the other, but we also have to fit a breath into our stroke. In order to maintain the correct neutral head position in Streamline, there is a limit to how far the body can rotate

Another factor to consider is how gravity affects an over-rotated body. When the body is over-rotated, the relationship between buoyancy and gravity changes. The over-rotated swimmer then has gravity working against them, causing the body to sink (see Figures 6.9a and 6.9b). This leaves the swimmer with only muscle power to create the rotation. This can become very tiring very quickly and would not be sustainable over long distances and certainly not in rough water.

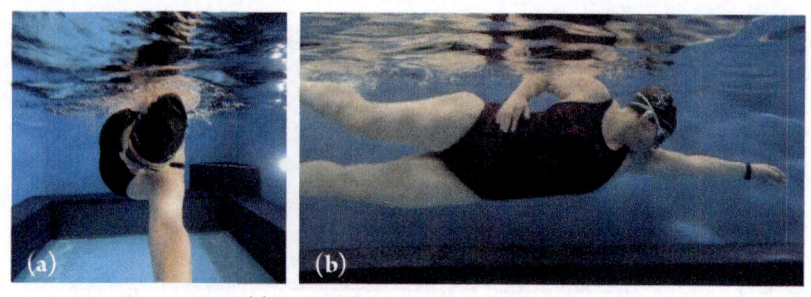

Figure 6.9: (a) Over-rotation causes the body to sink, and (b) Over-rotation causes the body to sink.

Figure 6.10: The correct streamline position.

The correct streamlined position in freestyle gives us the opportunity to tap into gravity to aid the invaluable weight shift. This only happens with a certain amount of rotation (see Figure 6.10) too little rotation and we haven't got enough angle to take advantage of; too much rotation and gravity has a negative effect on the body – it makes it sink, causing the limbs to try to stabilise the body to keep it at the surface. So, how do we find the right amount of rotation? This is closely linked to the overwater phase of the arm. We want to be able to recover our arm safely in the frontal plane, and the correct amount of rotation allows us to do this. We will cover this part of the stroke in Chapter 7.

Pool Activity 6.1 Finding streamline in the water

Just before beginning the following drill, it is good to practise Dryland Activity 6.1 again, standing in the water. This is a reminder to your body of the sensations you are looking for. Stand in the water using your scapular to send your cuticles towards the ceiling (*Build the Frame with Arms* position); go up onto the balls of your feet and swivel your belly button to the left, allowing the whole body to rotate towards the left. Ensure that your ribcage, pelvis, and legs rotate together, allowing your feet to swivel. Bring the left arm down to the moulded position that you practised in *Build the Frame with No Arms*, with your forearm just inside your front hip bone. Check that you are feeling the same sensations you discovered during the Dryland Activity. This will be your own feedback loop to ensure you have the right amount of rotation for your body.

6.1.1 Streamline

Push off in your *Build the Frame with Arms* position, and slide onto your 3 points of contact (see Figure 6.7b), sending your cuticles forwards and allowing the other arm to move to the moulded position. You will hit a moment of *Streamline* by doing this. It is your whole connected frame that rotates, from shoulders to feet; your head does not move. Your whole body will rotate back to flat almost immediately, and your legs may very quickly begin to sink: this is your cue to stand up and reset. Start to notice when this is happening so you can stand up a moment earlier whilst you are still rotated. Practise on one side, to begin with, so that you can give your body and your nervous system time to look for and find the same sensations you've experienced standing up. If you are finding it difficult to feel, it is always useful to rotate too far, reminding yourself of how that feels in the shoulder and neck area and how impossible it is to maintain your aligned head and your frame. This gives you a feedback loop that you can use to know when you've over-rotated.

When starting out with these practices, a good tip is to line yourself up with a marker on the bottom of the pool. It could be the black line or even just grout lines if the pool is tiled. Ensure you line up from head to feet with your marker and that your arm is running parallel to it. If there are no tiles or lines on the floor, sometimes you can see your shadow on the bottom of the pool from the pool lights above. This is another great way to ensure that you are lined up correctly. If you have an Endless Pool™ use the mirror on the bottom.

Once you've practised one side several times, practise the other and see if you can match the same sensation. Repeat the drill 3 – 4 times on each side, remembering that your aim is not to move along the pool but to feel positions. Therefore, take your time, and stand up between each repeat to refocus and reoxygenate.

Then, you need to integrate this into your whole stroke right away. So, push off into your *Build the Frame with Arms* position; immediately slide one scapula forward, allowing the other arm to mould to your body with your forearm just inside your front hip bone. Hit the *Streamline* position for a moment, and then continue with six strokes, hitting the *Streamline* position for a moment on every stroke you take. You can then repeat this exercise with three separate cues:

> - 3 points of contact
> - Lengthen through your middle trident prong
> - Lengthen alternately through your left/right trident prongs
>
> For each cue, follow this sequence:
> - stand-up rehearsal
> - 3 to 4 repeats of the drill
> - 3 repeats of 6 strokes without taking a breath
> - 3 to 4 single lengths (2 – 4 sets of 20 strokes if in an Endless Pool™). On these whole lengths, always perform the first 6 strokes without taking a breath to give your nervous system a moment to remember the sensation before you add in a breath.
>
> The discipline here is to ensure that you stick to the cue you are currently working on when you add in the breath. The temptation is to immediately switch focus to a breathing cue when adding inhalation. When executing the non-breathing strokes, remember to always bubble out through your nose and ensure you are not breath-holding.

You will know that you are in the correct *Streamline* position when:

- You are able to maintain your head to feet alignment
- You are able to maintain your frame from both shoulders to both feet as one unit
- Your *Streamline* arm is connected via the scapula to the torso, and you are able to send the cuticles forwards to the front wall
- Your other arm is moulded to your body, with your forearm just inside your front hip bone.

Figure 6.11: The correct streamline position from above the water.

To ensure that your frame is in place and you have the correct amount of rotation, use the following as a feedback loop. If you were lying on a flat surface in your right streamline position, your right pec, right hip bone and the front side of the right thigh would be making contact with it. These are your 3 points of contact. At the same time, on the left of the body, the left scapula will be brushing the surface, as will the top of the left buttock and the left hamstring. The waterline will be cutting the left upper arm in half (see Figure 6.11). If your entire left shoulder is out of the water, this indicates that you have pulled the arm and shoulder back behind the frontal plane, which impedes the movement of your scapula and limits your ability to recover your arm correctly in your next stroke. Chapter 7: Generate Forward Momentum looks at this in detail.

> ### Pool Activity 6.2 Streamline with flutter
>
> It is best practice to set the frame correctly every time by pushing off in *Build the Frame with Arms*. Practise the *Streamline* position by pushing off in this way and then moving into *Streamline* on one side. Maintain the shape either for as long as you can comfortably on one breath or until your feet start to sink, then stand up. Then, introduce a *Flutter* to the drill.

When performing *Streamline* with flutter, only introduce the Flutter once you have reached your now familiar *Streamline* position. This will mean that your whole body, from shoulders to feet, will have rotated at the same time to the same place, allowing the *Flutter* to be performed in the correct direction and plane. Visualise eight laser beams coming out of your body: two from your pecs, two from your hip bones, two from your knees and two from the front of your ankles, and ensure that all eight laser beams are pointing in the same direction (see Figure 6.12).

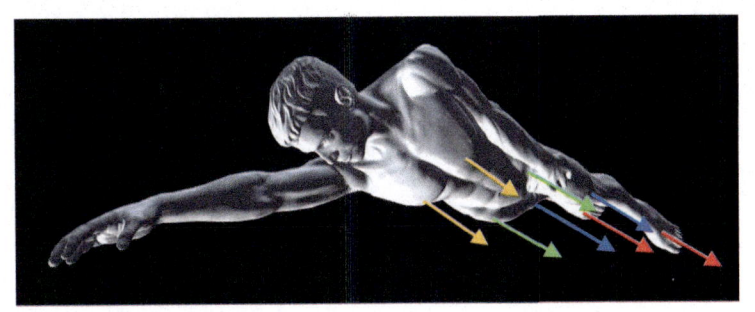

Figure 6.12: 8 laser beams showing a correctly aligned body in streamline.

When in *Streamline* we want the direction of the *Flutter* to be in the same direction as the rest of the body, at a slight diagonal. A common error, if a swimmer begins to *Flutter* in *Build the Frame with Arms* and then moves into the *Streamline* position, is that they leave their legs behind and *Flutter* in an up and down motion towards the ceiling and the bottom of the pool. You will notice that this points the pec and hip laser beams diagonally and the knee and ankle laser beams towards the floor (see Figure 6.13), causing a twist up the entire body and a complete loss of connection rather than allowing the legs to rotate with the rest of the body and stay connected.

The SwimMastery Way

Figure 6.13: 4 laser beams showing a correct upper body alignment and 4 incorrect lower body alignment in *Streamline*.

Summary of cues: Streamline

- » 3 points of contact
- » Whole body moves as one unit
- » Maintain middle trident
- » Use the scapula to send the cuticles to the far wall
- » Lengthen through your middle trident prong
- » Lengthen alternately through your left/right trident prongs
- » Flutter in the same direction as the rest of the body

Chapter 7

Generating forward momentum

Whilst I love talking about *Streamline* more than any other subject, I consider that *Generating Forward Momentum* is one of the most important aspects of freestyle, and the part of the stroke that traditional swimming and swim coaches pay very little attention to. It is almost as if 'out of sight is out of mind', but the consequences of poor or incorrect movements above the surface of the water are enormous. Let's explore why.

The first thing to think about is physics. When any part of the body is taken out of the water, it instantly becomes ten times heavier than it was when submerged. When swimming, there are also directional forces to consider. If you want to swim in a straight line, you need to send every movement of every body part in that same direction. With the added weight of the arm above the surface, and the ballistic forces involved in moving it, you must control the direction of movement, or you will be unable to control the direction that the energy moves in. A ballistic movement is an extremely rapid movement of the limbs which, once initiated, cannot be modified. Therefore, the arm recovery part of the stroke must be controlled as much as possible. Of course, this becomes more difficult at incredibly high tempos and speeds, making building the neurological pathways at slower tempos particularly important. Those pathways can then be relied on at the faster tempos.

We want to use the over-water phase of the arm movement, the recovery, as part of our lateral balance and stability, as we discussed in Chapter 1. If you send your arm out of the water behind you, up towards the ceiling or the sky, you are sending all that weight above your centre of gravity. Remember that as a rule of thumb, we always have 5% of the body out of the water and 95% of the body submerged, so sending the arm directly above the centre of gravity is going to take up most, if not all, of the 5%, causing the rest of the body to sink. This, in turn, will cause the body to feel unstable, and the swimmer will most likely try to brace with either the other arm and/or both legs. This instantly disconnects the limbs from the frame, causing the pelvis to move, and possibly even the head. This completely breaks the *Streamline* position at a time in the stroke when it is most critical to maintain it.

Of greater significance, taking the arm above the centre of gravity will put the shoulder girdle into a compromised and weak position, which, if repeated enough times, could lead to injury. We always want to ensure, first and foremost, that we are putting our joints into positions where they can get the strongest possible leverage, while minimising the risk of injury. We need to use the joints and muscles of the shoulder girdle from a position of strength. In order to tap into these correct joint movements, we have to ensure that the scapula is in the correct position and able to move freely.

Taking the elbow behind the swimmer towards the ceiling or the sky moves it closer to the spine and ribs and to its end range down the torso, causing the progress of the scapula to be impeded. This leaves the swimmer with only one way to get the arm forward of their head for the next stroke: to drop the elbow and bring the hand forward. This hand-led arm recovery can cause the swimmer to enter too far forward, swing the arm across their centreline, or swing the arm wide. This will send their energy to one side or the other instead of directly forwards and will almost always cause the depth of the *Streamline* arm to be incorrect. The deviations resulting from this disconnected overarm movement can lead to the swimmer covering much more lateral distance than they bargained for, taking up valuable time and using up valuable energy resources. The key to avoiding all these errors is ensuring that the pathway of the arm is correct.

We have already set up the position from which the arm exits the water, the place you returned your arm to in the *Streamline* drill, with the forearm lying just inside the front hip bone. There is a good reason for the temptation to pull that elbow back to clear the hand of the water: our human brains associate swimming with being on our fronts, i.e. flat, with no rotation.

There is an often-used phrase among swimmers around the world: the 'high elbow'. This arises from an obvious dilemma: if I am lying flat on my front, how can I take my hand out of the water and put it back in the water in front of my body without taking the entire arm behind my body? Of course, if you were indeed swimming flat, the answer is, that you can't. This incorrect movement, which we see in many swimmers across the globe, is an instinctual one. It is so hardwired into our nervous system, and it is quite literally outside the swimmer's visual field, that it takes enormous focus to break this pattern. A correct arm recovery with correct rotation creates an illusion of a high elbow; however, the high elbow is not created by lifting the elbow. Lifting your elbow during the arm recovery will result in inefficient stroke mechanics and eventually injury.

The first step towards breaking this pattern is to understand why humans instinctively do this in the first place; we need to understand why it is not necessary. We know that to keep the shoulder girdle safe and ensure that it is in a position of strength and

The SwimMastery Way

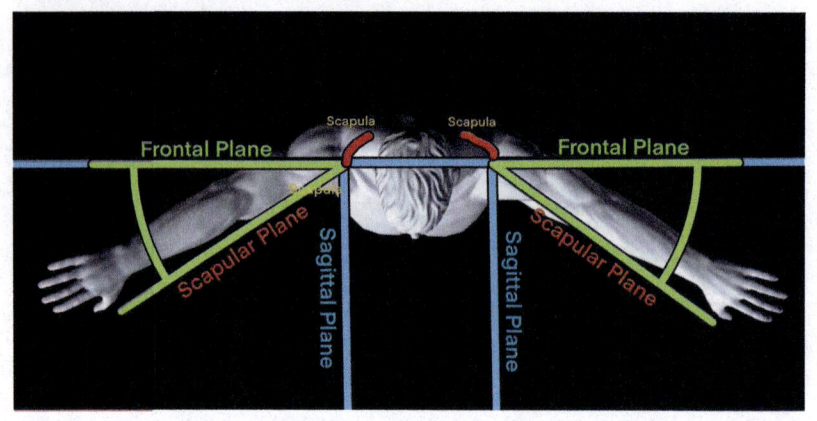

Figure 7.1: Position of Scapula and Frontal Planes.

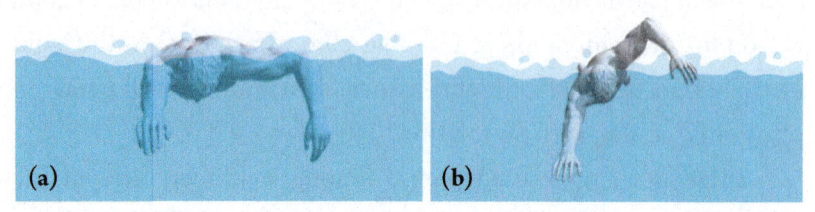

Figure 7.2: (a) Swimming flat keeping arm recovery within frontal plane, and (b) swimming with rotation keeping arm recovery within frontal plane.

avoid any chance of injury, we must keep the shoulder joint in front of the frontal plane (See Figure 7.1).

If we did swim flat on our fronts, then, of course, to maintain this position, we would have to keep the entire arm in the water as it moves forward; this would cause obvious amounts of resistance and no doubt some injury due to the resistance (see Figure 7.2a). But we are actually not swimming flat, and nor do we want to (see Figure 7.2b). As we've discussed in the *Streamline* section of this book, we want whole-body rotation in our stroke. This serves two purposes: it gives us the ability to use our available forces, i.e. gravity, to create the weight shift, and it also gives us space to recover the arm safely and with the least risk of the frame breaking during the process.

Generating forward momentum

Dry land activity 7.1

I recommend doing these standing rehearsals using at least one mirror, or preferably two. I am continually amazed at how our brain tells us we are doing something that bears no relation to what we are actually doing, especially with the arm recovery. The mirror(s) will allow you to know whether you are actually doing what you think you are doing.

7.1.1 Opening the gate

Stand in front of the first mirror; a second mirror will reflect you side-on. Step forward into a lunge position with your front leg bent and your back leg straight. Having one leg forward and one leg back should encourage a slight rotation in the body to simulate the rotation we have in *Streamline*. Support

Figure 7.3: Starting lunge position.

the weight of your body on the forward knee with your forearm (see Figure 7.3). Now tuck the other arm, which is straight, just inside your hip bone. Your hand will be hanging loosely on your inner thigh. Please note this will differ slightly for each individual, as arm lengths vary. What is important is that you feel that the shoulder is relaxed and not being held back, and you still have a slight rotation in your body.

Take the whole arm as one unit, and send the bone at the tip of your elbow directly out to the side, as if opening a gate

The SwimMastery Way

Figure 7.4: (a) Open the gate front on and (b) Open the gate rear view.

(see Figures 7.4 a and b). Then return the arm to the starting position, as if closing the gate. It is not a big movement, and it should be fluid, easy and comfortable. Repeat this movement several times, opening and closing.

I would now like you to experience a poor but common arm recovery movement pattern so you have a comparison to the correct movement. Do not perform this movement if you have a current or historic shoulder injury. Start in the same lunge position and send your elbow back behind you. Notice the difference you feel in your body with this movement as you send the shoulder joint behind the scapular plane (see Figure 7.5).

Figure 7.5: Elbow back.

Now go back to the correct movement, and notice the difference that you feel, particularly around the scapula. Can you feel how the scapula and shoulder joint articulate very smoothly when taking the elbow to the side wall, compared with how the scapula and the shoulder joint articulate when you take the elbow behind you towards the ceiling? Repeat both these movements a few times very slowly so you can learn the sensations for both. Of course, I don't want you to imprint the incorrect movement, so this will be the only time that you execute this pulling back of the elbow. Still, it is an excellent way to tune your body and nervous system into what it should feel like when you're doing it correctly, versus what it feels like when done incorrectly. It is your own personal feedback loop.

Switch to the other side and repeat the correct and incorrect movements as above.

Now that you have found your feedback loop and the sensations that you feel with the correct movement are becoming familiar, I would like you to practise the following on both sides. From your starting point, send the elbow out to the side, allowing the forearm from the elbow down to simply hang from the elbow; your hand will be directly beneath your elbow (see Figure 7.6). Then, return your arm to the starting point. Can you feel how the arm is still connected to the scapula, as we spoke about in *Build the Frame with Arms* and the Streamline position? As you open the gate, the scapula slides forwards; as you close the gate, the scapula slides backwards, all the while maintaining the body rotation that you started with. Once you feel this sensation of the scapula and arm being connected and it all being one continuous movement, you can move on to the next step. Something

Figure 7.6: Lower arm hanging off the elbow.

to watch out for during this part of the exercise is to make sure that you are not rolling the shoulder down. If we roll the shoulder down, we will end up with the elbow pointing backwards, and you will then not be able to execute the rest of the arm recovery pathway correctly.

7.1.2 Tattoo forward

For the next step, we are simply going to continue this movement for longer. To do this, with my clients, I often use the analogy of a tattoo, and ask clients to imagine they have a tattoo on this soft tissue, and they are going to move it forward. Now using your finger, find the outer end of the crease in your elbow, take your finger just below that, and press into the soft tissue (see Figure 7.7). This is the point you are now going to continue to send forwards following from opening the gate. While executing this movement, the arm from the elbow down is completely relaxed and just hanging. Again, it is important

Generating forward momentum

to remember this is one fluid movement. We are simply continuing on from what we did before. Also, notice that once again, the entire scapula and arm move as one unit.

As you slide the scapula and the arm forward, the muscles attached to the scapula are lengthening and engaging. By focusing on moving the scapula, we automatically engage the muscles that are needed. I often hear swim coaches and swimmers talking about individual muscles, the latissimus dorsi (the 'lats') being one that is frequently mentioned when discussing the arm recovery. And while, of course, we want the 'lats' to be engaged, there are many more muscles that are required to execute the movement correctly, safely and powerfully. If you focus simply on trying to engage or lengthen your 'lats', there is a good chance you will overdo the movement and send the arm in the wrong direction to '**feel**' the 'lat'. By focusing on sliding the scapula and the arm as one unit, we are looking to engage what needs to be engaged as a by-product of this movement. It is important to note that this is a straight line movement; you will have no curving outwards or inwards. You are opening the gate and sending the tattoo forwards in a straight line. The forearm is just hanging. It should feel comfortable and easy to do.

Figure 7.7: Position of tattoo.

If performed correctly, the above exercises will no doubt feel completely different from any arm recovery movement you have done before. This is a good thing. Often, when we change a movement because it is different to what our nervous system knows, it can feel very strange and even incorrect. This is not because it is incorrect but simply because it is different. In order to imprint this new movement into the nervous system, you will have to tap into that sensation of it feeling strange or even incorrect to ensure that you are making the change. This acts as a feedback loop: if it feels normal, then you are probably doing what you have always done, and therefore you are not making the necessary changes. Awareness and ownership of this new sensation are what will help you make the biggest changes as quickly as possible.

7.1.3 Cuckoo

If you have practised the second step above correctly, you will automatically end this movement at the correct entry point for you. The scapula and arm slide forwards in a straight line. Once they can no longer slide in a straight line, you have reached the natural entry point (Figure 7.8a). If you were to continue this scapula and arm movement, one of two things would happen: either you would start to internally rotate the arm and send it across your centre line, or you would be moving the hand and forearm in isolation, causing an overreaching entry and loss of connection of the arm to the torso. Learning to feel the scapula and arm moving as one unit will be vital to you finding your personal entry point.

Now create a feedback loop to ensure you have your arm in the correct position. Once you have slid the scapula and

Generating forward momentum

Figure 7.8: Cuckoo (entry) position.

arm forwards to that natural entry point, you should be able to rotate your head and look under your arm. The arm should be framing your head in this position. We call this the '*Cuckoo*' position, because as you turn your head, you can say '*Cuckoo*' under your arm. Note that this position is not in any way connected to breathing; it is just a check in to use during your standing rehearsal (see Figure 7.8b). Again, it should feel comfortable, albeit probably different from what you are used to. Practise this position on both sides.

Generate forward momentum in the water

You are going to practise the arm recovery cues in whole stroke. Circling through each of the cues in whole stroke will give you a chance to imprint each of them sequentially.

It is good practice with any learning to be able to recognise the moment the sensation is changing and to be able to stop and reset before you lose the correct sensation until you can reset during the stroke. This way, you will imprint only the positive sensation into your nervous system, myelinating those neural pathways and making them stronger more quickly.

> ### Pool Activity 7.1 Whole-Stroke Practice
>
> As with the other exercises, I highly recommend executing a few stand-up rehearsals in the pool before starting the drills. Here, you are reminding yourself of the sensation of the correct movement of sending your arm away from you and forwards, instead of backwards and behind you. Then push off in your *Build the Frame with Arms* into your *Streamline* position, remembering that this is a great way to start each practice as your nervous system will recognise the stable platform from previous practice sessions. We assume the swimmer has imprinted the correct amount of rotation into their nervous system before working on the arm recovery to perform the arm recovery movement safely and correctly.
>
> #### 7.1.1 Open the gate
>
> Remember this is whole stroke and *Open the gate* is your cue. Starting in left *Streamline*

position, you are going to open your right gate and stroke into right *Streamline*, open the gate with your left and stroke into left Streamline, and so on. Continue for 6 strokes without taking a breath, then stand up. Repeat this 4 times before moving on to the next cue, as getting this first movement right will determine whether the next can be right. If you have taken the elbow back behind the scapular plane, the scapula can no longer slide forward. Start the repeats with alternate right and left arms. Then add in breathing, maintaining focus on the *Open the gate cue*.

This *Open the gate* cue tends to be the one that feels the strangest when you first start. Over the years clients have said that they feel like they are a bear, a sumo wrestler or a crab; their arms feel very wide because they have previously spent so much time trying to keep them in tight. Remind yourself that the arm must go wide to keep your shoulder joint safe and to aid lateral balance and weight shift through gravity.

Once you are consistently able to send your elbow out wide at the first point of exiting the water, you will no longer need to use this cue and can initiate the arm recovery with the *Tattoo forward* cue.

7.1.2 Tattoo forward

Once you have practised the *Open the gate* cue several times, move on to the next cue. Press your finger into the tattoo area several times to remind yourself where it is. As in the dryland rehearsal, you are going to send your tattoo forwards. From your *Streamline* position, slide the scapula and arm forward in one fluid movement, remembering

The SwimMastery Way

that you are not taking the hand forward but the tattoo. Feel the scapula and arm move forwards in the direction of travel. Swim six strokes with this cue with no breathing, and then stand up. Repeat this 4 times, starting with alternate right and left arms. Then add in breathing, maintaining focus on the *Tattoo forward* cue.

Over time, you will begin to notice that you will only need to use this cue to perform the correct arm recovery. What will change is that you will start to think about the cue *Tattoo forward* from the beginning of the arm recovery and no longer need to use *Open the gate*. This will help create a seamless arm recovery that travels forwards, generating forward momentum.

If I had to choose one cue that would impact a swimmer's stroke most, I would choose *Tattoo forward*.

7.1.3 Cuckoo and Entry

Once you have practised the above, you should now consistently be reaching your perfect entry point. You can now think about using your whole body rotation to send the entering *Cuckoo* arm to your *Streamline* position in one movement. The cuticles reach their destination at exactly the same time as you hit the three points of contact in *Streamline*. This results in one fluid movement of the arm recovery from exit to *Streamline*, ensuring that the rotation of the whole body once at the *Cuckoo* position sends the arm to *Streamline*. Please note there is no pause at *Cuckoo*: it is one fluid movement.

Swim six strokes with this cue with no breathing, and then stand up. Repeat this 4 times, starting with alternate right and left arms. Then add in breathing, maintaining focus on the *Cuckoo* cue.

7.1.4 Fingers in the water

Keeping your fingers in the water as you are sending your *Tattoo forward* will greatly aid this process. To begin with, this will be a separate cue, and it will give you a feedback loop to let your brain know where your hand actually is. Ask yourself for honest feedback when trying this out the first few times. Can you definitely feel your fingers in the water? If you can't, that simply means that your fingers are not in the water! Repeat the exercise until you feel your fingers are wet throughout the six strokes. I find it fascinating how long this process can take; it is a reminder to us that we must stay true to the cue at hand rather than working on a cue but not actually getting the feedback. Attention to this kind of detail will help you improve these movements more quickly. Using an 'attention to detail' score can be helpful with this, as described in Chapter 2.

Feeling your fingers in the water is an opportunity for a feedback loop and not the end result. As you practise the cues in whole-stroke and your movements become more fluid, you will start to notice that your fingers just skim the surface of the water and eventually end up just millimetres above it.

You have now practised the four cues:
- open the gate
- take the tattoo forwards
- cuckoo to streamline
- fingers in the water

As you move through this sequence of cues, incrementally increase the difficulty by adding more repeats with breathing.

As with other practices, I suggest always starting off the length with six strokes without breathing and then carrying on swimming the length, adding in breathing but maintaining your focus on your chosen cue.

> **Summary of cues: Generate Forward Momentum**
>
> » Open the gate
> » Tattoo forward
> » Cuckoo to streamline
> » Fingers in the water

Chapter 8

Stroke synchronisation

So far, through the process, we have simply been connecting the body - creating a single unit. I learnt from Terry Laughlin a principle passed to him from Bill Boomer, former US Olympic Swim Coach, that "The shape of the vessel matters more than the size of the engine". A key feature of the shape of the vessel is its length. You started creating a longer vessel by connecting your legs to your torso through the pelvis and getting your head on right. Next, you attached your arms to your torso through the scapula, creating an even longer vessel. You then learned to maintain this long vessel while you moved one of your arms forwards above the water. You will now learn how to continue to maintain this long vessel as you switch from one side to the other. This is where the magic happens!

When we talk about stroke timing, we are essentially talking about synchronising every single part of the stroke. The end goal is to achieve one simultaneous movement of the whole body.

Losing connections

As terrestrial mammals, we have an inbuilt survival instinct when immersed in water, as explained in Chapter 1. This instinct becomes strongly evident when we begin to address stroke timing, because swimmers have an innate urge to pull or paddle with their arms in the water in an attempt to ensure they can keep their head above or as close to the surface as possible. But this very act of pulling or paddling instantly disconnects the arms from the torso. This disconnection removes our ability to access bigger muscle groups, resulting in the smaller, unstable muscles around the shoulder girdle being used, leading to injury and fatigue. Working in isolation, smaller muscles will fatigue much faster than larger, connected muscle groups. This act of pulling or paddling also creates two types of resistance in the water. It creates form drag because the arms are no longer connected and no longer create a long vessel. It also creates wave drag because the disconnected arm moves the water, and we cannot hold on to moving water. Chapter 10 on *Catch* will look more closely at holding on to the water.

Dead spots

Have you ever been at the pool, looked across the lane next to you, and seen a swimmer moving seamlessly through the water with no splash or noise? They seem to flow through the water effortlessly, in one continuous motion. It is a thing of beauty and something we all strive to achieve. There is nothing better than being tapped on the shoulder by another swimmer in the pool, having them tell you that they love your stroke, and asking where you learned it. This very scenario happened to one of my swimmers recently, and he was beaming with joy as he told me about the conversation. Seamless swimming is noticeable, and this perpetual motion of the stroke will make you the most efficient swimmer.

However, it is very common to see swimmers with lots of dead spots or deceleration points, in pools around the world. Any part of the stroke that causes you to decelerate, even a little, is an area to work on. Let's consider three common areas where dead spots occur.

During the breath

Because of our survival instinct, creating a dead spot during the breath is very easy. Swimmers often turn towards the air too late, causing them to lift their head too far out of the water and press down with the *Streamline* arm. At this moment, physics is working against the swimmer because the weight of the head coming up out of the water (8% of body weight) causes the rest of the body to start sinking down towards the bottom of the pool. The *Streamline* arm creates a bracing motion to try to counter this (usually subconscious) sinking feeling. This only serves to make the swimmer sink further downward because they have changed their direction of travel from forwards to downwards and upwards. The swimmer will often also brace with the legs and splay them in an attempt to stabilise the body during the breathing stroke. All of these stabilising movements cause a huge amount of resistance in the water and result in deceleration at that moment. Chapter 9, on *Integrated Breathing,* introduces strategies that will reduce the likelihood of dead spots occurring here.

During the switch point

Stroke timing, or synchronisation, is the most important part of the learning cycle to enable you to achieve the magic of perpetual motion. Many drills have been created to help swimmers achieve a perfectly timed stroke, but we often see swimmers switching either too early or too late.

Windmilling, where a swimmer spins both arms in an attempt to generate and maintain perpetual forward motion, is one strategy that can work for short distances, although it is very tiring and inefficient.

The opposite of this, where the swimmer glides out in front for too long, looks almost like a catch-up stroke: the swimmer hits their *Streamline* position and then waits in that *Streamline* position for too long, usually until the other arm has already entered the water. They then have to rely on a big, explosive pull and kick to get them round and forward to the next *Streamline* position. This hugely decelerates the stroke and requires the swimmer to rely on smaller muscles to get them round to the next *Streamline*. This is also very tiring and inefficient.

You may be using stroke count as a way to measure your progress in the pool. When looking for the right switch point, it's important to remember that you should not be striving for your lowest possible stroke count but for the perfect combination of stroke count, tempo and rate of perceived effort (RPE), as we outline in Chapter 13, Speed.

At the beginning of rotation

Another common point of deceleration is at the moment when a swimmer is about to begin their rotation. They wind up their body, ready to fire round into their next *Streamline* position. What often happens then is that the body over-rotates as one leg pulls back and the *Catch* arm gets ready to apply pressure. The swimmer then fires and shoots forward into the next stroke. This causes increased resistance, and deceleration as a result.

Maintaining connections

Synchronising every part of the stroke requires whole-stroke practice, focusing on different elements of the stroke one at a time until the nervous system can imprint these new synchronisation points and perform them all together. As our awareness and understanding of the stroke and our proprioception improve, so too does our ability to achieve this goal.

The first part of the stroke that we want to time together is the whole-body rotation sending the *Cuckoo* arm to *Streamline*. The important thing to remember is that we do not want to compromise the connections we have already set when performing the dynamic weight shift of each stroke. During all the upcoming exercises, it is vital you remember your non-negotiable *Frame*, i.e. head-to-foot line. If you feel your *Frame* needs some attention before attempting these synchronisation points, revisit the exercises in Chapter 4, *Build the Frame*, thinking about the body as a trident. The middle prong of the trident travels straight down the centre of the body from the feet to the head, with two side prongs travelling through both scapulae to the cuticles. Once we have set out the trident through our *Build the Frame* and *Streamline* positions, we then corkscrew our trident along the length of the pool, lake, or ocean that we are swimming in. The key is always to take the path of least resistance with every stroke while maintaining a connected body. Through this connected body, we access the maximum amount of power for the least effort whilst creating the least resistance.

The second part of the stroke to synchronise is timing both arms to the rotation; to do this, we're going to focus on both scapulae. If our setup position is correct on both the *Streamline* side and on the side of the recovery arm, then, at that moment of weight shift, both scapulae should be forward. At the moment of the weight shift, the top scapula (the *Cuckoo* arm side) sends the cuticles forward down the pool.

Dryland activity 8.1 Stroke Synchronisation

8.1.1 Rotate cuticles forward

Get into the left lunge position that you used when practising the arm recovery in the previous chapter, Generating Forward Momentum. Ensure that you have the correct body rotation, and then send your right scapula and arm forward to the *Cuckoo* position you are familiar with. Once you have checked your *Cuckoo* position, step forward with your right leg as if stepping forward into a lunge on the right side. At exactly the same time that you step forward, simply straighten the *Cuckoo* arm, sending your cuticles forwards towards the wall in front of you. Then go back to your starting point and practise this timing again. The rotation of the body and straightening of the arm are simultaneous movements, triggered in this rehearsal by stepping forward. The act of stepping forward mimics your whole body rotation, and it is this rotation that will straighten the *Cuckoo* arm to its *Streamline* position. The arm does not move in isolation. Once you've practised this several times on this side, practise the same timing on the other side.

8.1.2 Keep the scapula forward

Once you've practised this on both sides a few times, turn your attention to the scapula. Go through the same movement, and as you take the step forward, notice that the scapula remains forward and connected to the *Cuckoo* arm during its journey to extension. This is a key element in the stroke, as what often happens is that people drop their elbows as they extend. Through this elbow drop, the scapula slides backwards and the connection of the torso to the arm is lost. As soon as that connection is lost, you instantly shorten your vessel and lose your opportunity to harness the body's more efficient and stronger muscle systems. As you step forward, keep your attention on maintaining the scapula position all the way through to extension. Practise this exercise with this new focus several times on each side. Once you are able to maintain the scapula position and simply straighten the arm as you step forward, you will notice that your arm always goes to the same place by default.

Pool activity 8.1 Synchronisation in the water

You are now going to practise your stroke synchronisation in the water. First, I would like you to do six strokes without taking a breath, just tuning in to what you currently feel. Do you get some sense of what happens to your connections as you dynamically weight-shift from your left to your right? Check the tiles on the floor of the pool, or something on the bottom of the lake, to give yourself a measure of your forward momentum. You're going to use this measure for comparison when you start to focus on your stroke synchronisation cues. Do this a few times, notice how far you travelled over the six strokes, and how the water felt around your body as you switched.

8.1.1 Whole-body rotation sends *Cuckoo* arm to *Streamline*

In this practice, you will be synchronising movements on the same side of the body. Just before beginning the new cues, repeat the rehearsal that you practised in your lunge position, straightening your *Cuckoo* arm to *Streamline* as you take a small step forward to lunge on the other side; this is a reminder of what you felt as you straightened the arm. Now do six strokes focusing on the whole body sending your *Cuckoo* arm to *Streamline*. The instant that your recovery arm hits its *Cuckoo* position, you are going to rotate your body and straighten the arm to your perfect *Streamline* position.

Sometimes we need to break this down a little further, and even though we are doing six strokes - left, right, left, right, left, right - it is sometimes necessary to just focus on each right-side synchronisation, i.e. every 2nd stroke, and then repeat just focusing on every left-side stroke. As with the dryland rehearsal, at the moment of weight shift, it is essential to ensure that the scapula and upper arm maintain their position. If this has been performed correctly, your stroke will be silent and create no splash or bubbles. However, if at that moment of weight shift you lose the connection by allowing the elbow to drop and consequently the scapula to slide backwards, it will create a kerplunk noise as the elbow smacks the water. This is a great feedback loop to tune in to! Another feedback loop that you can rely on during this part of the synchronisation is based on the familiarity with the correct *Streamline* position that you have developed through your practice from previous chapters. If you have maintained the connection of the arm through the scapula to the torso and you simply rotate and straighten the arm from the *Cuckoo* position, it will always extend to the correct depth. Remember, if the *Cuckoo* position is correct, it is the rotation that sends the cuticles to the correct depth. There is never any need to consciously direct the arm. To begin with when you work on these synchronisation points, it may feel a little robotic; with practice, the end result should feel relaxed and fluid.

Once you have practised this enough to ensure that the connection has been maintained and that the synchronisation has happened correctly, see if you can add a few integrated breaths, maintaining the focus on the synchronisation. You are aiming to create the same fluid sensation with and without that integrated breath.

Trident

It is easy to get too focused on positions and forget that our aim is to move down the pool or across a lake. So, once you have the *Cuckoo arm to Streamline* synchronisation point well established, you need to work on integrating it with sending energy forward through each of the 3 prongs of your *Trident*. Think about where you are directing all of the energy that you are generating: incorporate the *Trident* cues (discussed in previous chapters) into your synchronisation practice. Harnessing generated power in the right direction in this way will result in a reduced stroke count and increased speed.

Pool activity 8.2 Trident

8.2.1 Middle prong

For this exercise, on the first repeat of six strokes, I would like you to use the whole body rotation to send the *Cuckoo* arm into *Streamline*, and this time send the middle prong of your *Trident* forward. While you are rotating into the next stroke, you are lengthening your whole body through the top of your head. This is the most important part of the body to lengthen through, as it helps us to maintain our non-negotiable head to feet line. Most swimmers are prone to lengthening through the lead arm, causing over-extension, disconnection and, therefore, over-rotation in the body. This sends the energy spinning round rather than sending the swimmer forwards.

8.2.2 Low prong

Now, keeping the same focus on using your whole body to send the *Cuckoo* arm to extension, focus on lengthening through that same side scapula, i.e. low side of the *Trident*.

The SwimMastery Way

As you do this, notice what you feel in your body. Are you over-extending because you are stretching the arm forward, or are you just lengthening through that scapula? If you are practising in a swimming pool, you can use the tiles to give you feedback; if you are overextending and stretching through the arm, it is very likely that you are going to move laterally as well as forwards. Lining yourself up along a grout line or a tile line helps to give you concrete feedback on your direction of movement.

8.2.3 High prong

Next, using energy generated by the whole body rotation, you are going to lengthen through the third prong of your Trident, which is now the top scapula. Sending the energy forward through this top scapula helps to stop you from pulling that scapula backwards at the moment of full extension, which is a very common error we see in swimmers. Focusing on this part of the stroke is usually quite a revelation to swimmers as they feel very stable doing this, and they can see that it maintains a full forward direction of energy during the weight shift (see Figure 8.1a).

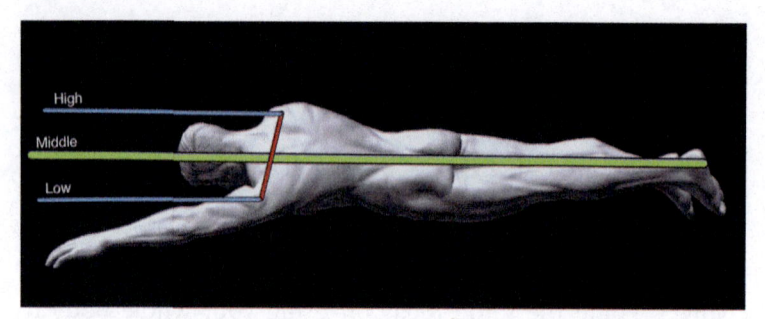

Figure 8.1a: Middle, Low and High trident prongs in *Streamline*.

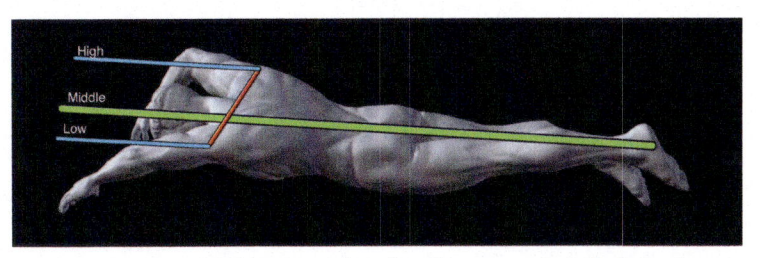

Figure 8.1b: Middle, Low and High trident prong in Whole stroke.

Once you have spent time practising channelling energy through each of the prongs individually, you can blend these cues. Start with middle and low *Trident* prongs together on both sides, and then middle and high *Trident* prongs together on both sides. Finally, try channelling the energy through all 3 *Trident* prongs together.

Summary of cues: Stroke Synchronisation:

» Whole-body rotation sends *Cuckoo* arm to extension
» Rotate cuticles forward
» Channel energy through the middle prong
» Channel energy through the low prong
» Channel energy through the high prong
» Channel energy through the middle and low prongs
» Channel energy through the middle and high prongs
» Channel energy through the middle, low and high prongs

Chapter 9

Integrated Breathing

The idea of how to breathe whilst swimming often fills swimmers with dread. "I would like to learn how to breathe" are the words I have heard from swimmers more than any other at the beginning of the many workshops I have run over the years. Being able to breathe is essential to survival, and breathing efficiently in the freestyle stroke is particularly challenging.

The human head constitutes 8% of the body by weight. When one considers how small the head is in relation to the rest of the body, this is surprising - imagine trying to swim while pushing a watermelon along in front of you! The challenge is significant when we couple this with the instinctive need for air, requiring the head to swivel. Regardless of how efficiently we learn to breathe, there will always be some level of lateral movement when we turn our heads to the air because the head we are moving forward is a heavy weight.

If the swimmer has spent enough time building their ideal *Frame* and *Streamline* position and is able to maintain those during the arm recovery phase of the stroke, they will have a stable enough platform from which to breathe. With the body in the right alignment, we simply breathe at the point in our stroke where it is most efficient - a position we have discussed throughout the book. This is the *Streamline* position, with the head turned towards the air.

The trick is being able to take a breath while changing nothing other than the head position.

Working with the water

When we are swimming forwards we are moving water out of the way, just as a boat does. This causes the water to rise up in front of the head, forming a bow wave with a trough between the head and the crest of the wave. For a swimmer with an aligned head, the crest of the bow wave dips down alongside the mouth, so this is the ideal place to take a breath. However, due to the human need for air, swimmers often lift or tilt their head in an attempt to find it. If this happens, for example, if they are looking over their shoulder or backwards, their nose would be in the trough of the bow wave, keeping their mouth in the water, leaving them with no alternative but to lift their head to get air (see Figure 9.1). There are three elements to integrated breathing to take advantage of the bow wave. The most important is the timing of the breath. Then comes

Figure 9.1: Lifting the head and looking back on a breath.

Integrated Breathing

the body position during the breath; thirdly, we exercise good air management (Chapter 3: Air Exchange).

Timing of the breath

Almost without exception, every swimmer instinctively turns their head too late to the breath. There is a very good reason for this. At the ideal moment that we should take the breath, our body should be in the *Streamline* position. Imagine you are going to take a left-side breath. The correct moment to start allowing the head to move round to the air is at the moment of the weight shift or the rotation, but at this moment, the left arm is still extended as part of my left side *Streamline* (see Figure 9.2). This position creates a subconscious thought process in the brain: "I can't possibly allow my head to turn to the air now because there is an arm in the way". So the brain typically waits a moment until that *Streamline* arm has moved and it feels comfortable enough to allow the head to turn to the air. But this results in a breath that is far too late, missing the bow wave and having to distort the body position to reach for air, usually by lifting the head and pressing downwards on the leading arm. This, in turn, makes for a very different movement on each breathing stroke to

Figure 9.2: Start allowing the head to move.

the previously-imprinted non-breathing stroke, and causes a limp in the stroke on each breath, which takes one or two strokes to recover from and realign. The rhythmic, smooth and aligned swimming motion is lost.

One very simple fix to try in the pool is to cue 'turn your head earlier to the breath'. This often works well and results in the swimmer feeling as though they have more space and time to breathe. As explained in the previous chapter on synchronisation, the moment of the weight shift is where all the magic happens. The magic of the breath happens here too!

Let's break down the timing of this movement a little further. To recap, we want the body in a perfect *Streamline* position and to be able to maintain that *Streamline* position during the entire recovery phase up to the *Cuckoo* position. It is at this moment that we are going to allow the head to move with the next body rotation. As we know, the *Cuckoo* position, in the right place, at the right time, sends enough weight forwards to allow gravity to start the next stroke naturally, i.e. the beginning of the rotation. The rotation sends the recovering arm to its *Streamline* position and simultaneously, we allow the head to move round with the rotation towards the air. It is at that moment of weight shift that we create the most propulsion, and, therefore, it is the moment where the body is highest in the water. Due to the speeds that most recreational swimmers achieve, this extra height is marginal, but, nevertheless, it is there - and it is at this moment that we take full advantage of the bow wave that is created through this phase. Any later, the bow wave will have collapsed, and we will need to lift our head higher to get to the air. If we are able to inhale in the trough of the bow wave we are, essentially, breathing lower than the surface of the water and that is the ideal moment. It is therefore the only moment where we can achieve an ideal head position. If we miss this moment, we have to lift the head or press the arm to get to the air.

Body position

We need to maintain the body positions we have already learnt: the frame, a neutral head before, during, and after the breath, and a connected *Streamline* arm. This is, of course, easier said than done, as the brain usually kicks into survival mode at the mere mention of the word breathing, and, therefore, this requires a lot of attention. It is why we spend so much time during the early stages of learning, practising the skills without breathing, to give the nervous system an opportunity to imprint and recognise these positions before adding in the breath.

At the moment of weight shift, the rotation simultaneously sends the *Cuckoo* arm to extension and sends the aligned head round to the air, leaving the swimmer in a perfect *Streamline* position, with the stability that comes with that while they are breathing (see Figure 9.3). It is essential that the head remains

Figure 9.3: Head at the air in *Streamline*.

aligned and merely turns as it goes round to the air. A common error that is often seen in swimmers, and, sadly, often taught, is to look over the shoulder during the breath as if that is where there is more air. The obvious problem this causes is that it sends the head out of alignment and will result in a lateral deviation and a loss of the all-important and non-negotiable frame. Remembering that our head is 8% of our body weight, it is clear that there would be an undesirable knock-on effect of moving this weight in the wrong direction while we are in an unstable medium. Lifting the head can cause loss of connection in the *Streamline* arm, between the rib cage and the pelvis, and in the hip flexors; the legs then tend to move into a bracing position to help the body to feel, or find, stability lost through the head lift.

To summarise, to maintain a stable and *Streamline* frame, the ideal position is for the swimmer to see directly towards the side, where the bow wave dip is.

Air exchange

By the time you have come to integrating your breathing position into the stroke, you should be very familiar with your air exchange cycle. You will now need to incorporate the air exchange cycle you have been using up until now into the breathing cycle within your stroke. As soon as your face enters the water you begin a slow controlled exhale, out through the nose. When you begin to turn the head to the breath with the whole-body rotation, you will begin a more explosive exhale, again out through the nose. And then, as soon as your mouth clears the water in the trough of the bow wave, you will allow a diaphragmatic inhale to take place. Then you return your head before repeating this cycle for the next breath.

Head return

I have frequently heard people talk about timing the breath, saying that you turn your head on one hand entry, and return it on the next. However, this would result in the head being in the breathing position for far too long, interrupting the timing of the stroke and limiting scapula movement during the arm recovery. We have to continually take into account that the head is 8% of our body weight. Therefore, any movement of that head, because it is out in front and moving through water, is going to disrupt the forward momentum of the body. When we turn our head to breathe, it changes the profile that we present to the water, so keeping the head in the breathing position for longer than necessary will cause more lateral deviation. We want to minimise the disruption as much as possible by keeping the head in the breathing position only for as long as necessary. We do not want to be able to see our recovering arm passing by our head whilst we are breathing. This would be a clear indication that your breath is too late and the head has stayed there for too long.

The biggest opportunity for improvement here comes from decoupling the head return and the arm entry. We are looking for the head to return to neutral as an independent movement. This is a tricky concept because we want the head-turn to be coupled to the whole-body rotation and arm entry on the way to the breath, but returning from the breath, we want to uncouple the head-turn from the rotation and arm. This will no doubt feel very discombobulated. To experience similar discombobulation, pat your head and rub your tummy at the same time, as I am sure you have done many times before; now, switch your hands around. This is a similar sensation to when you first practise this early head return. Stick with it – keep practising - your brain will adapt to the skill, and it will feel easier.

Dryland activity 9.1 Integrated breathing

It is very helpful to do this in front of a mirror to ensure you have the correct alignment. To start with, you're going to focus on the Cuckoo position and the timing of the breath. You will bring in the other arm later.

9.1.1 From cuckoo position to the air

During this rehearsal we are going to connect up 4 parts of the stroke.

Standing up, with your feet hip distance apart, go up onto the balls of your feet and swivel your whole body (8 laser beams, see Chapter 6 Streamline Figure 6.6) to the left-hand

Figure 9.4: (a) *Streamline* and (b) *Cuckoo*.

corner of the room, maintaining visual contact with yourself in the mirror, or a fixed point on the wall in front of you. Lower your heels.

In this slightly rotated position, with a neutral head, bring your left arm up into the *Cuckoo* position (see Figure 9.4 a and b). Then, go back onto the balls of your feet, and simultaneously:

» swivel your whole body (8 laser beams) to the right corner of the room
» straighten your *Cuckoo* arm
» send your fingernails directly to the ceiling
» allow the head to rotate round with your whole body.

You will finish in your left *Streamline* position, with your head looking towards the wall on your right. This is your breathing position.

Return to the starting position and repeat this movement on the same side several times until you can feel that all the movements are happening simultaneously: it becomes one movement with everything happening at the same time. Then, switch sides and practise the same thing to the other side. It is imperative that we practise both breathing sides equally. Notice the comparative fluidity of the two sides; if one is less fluid, use the more fluid side as the model to help the other learn to become more comfortable.

9.1.2 Timing the breath with both arms

Once the above exercise feels fluid and easy, start again, and this time, use both arms to rehearse the whole stroke. Start in the same position and swivel to the left, ensuring the torso and feet are rotated, the head has remained neutral by looking in the mirror or at your fixed point, and the left arm is in the *Cuckoo* position. Now put your right arm into its *Streamline* position, with fingernails touching the ceiling as an extension of the scapula, as in *Build the frame* with arms and *Streamline*. Next, as you swivel your whole body, allowing the head to go along for the ride, extend your left *Cuckoo* arm to the ceiling and allow the right *Streamline*

Figure 9.5: Integrated Breathing Standing Rehearsal sequence.

arm to drop down and the forearm to plant itself just inside the left hip bone, finishing in your left *Streamline* position with your head looking towards the side wall. This is your breathing position. (See Figure 9.5). Remember that this is all one movement. Then return head back to the starting, neutral position before rehearsing the next breath. Be sure to practise this equally on both sides.

Pool activity 9.1 Integrated breathing

As with all the other exercises, once you get into the water, remind the body of the movement pattern by going through the dryland rehearsal.

We are now going to break this down into 4 steps. Ideally, you will be slowly exhaling from your nose during the exercises in all three steps, but you will not focus on this until 9.1.3.

9.1.1 Timing

You are not trying to get a breath yet; you are simply practising the timing of the head turn. Because you are not concerned with having to get air, you will be more able

Integrated Breathing

to concentrate on and stick to the cue at hand. Push off in your *Build the Frame* position and begin by taking two slow, controlled, non-breathing strokes. On the 3rd stroke, allow your head to rotate with the whole body at the moment of weight shift, and then let the head return to neutral. This will result in you ending this exercise in your *Streamline* position. Then, stand up and repeat. (See Figure 9.6) At first, stopping in the *Streamline* position is very tricky as the body wants

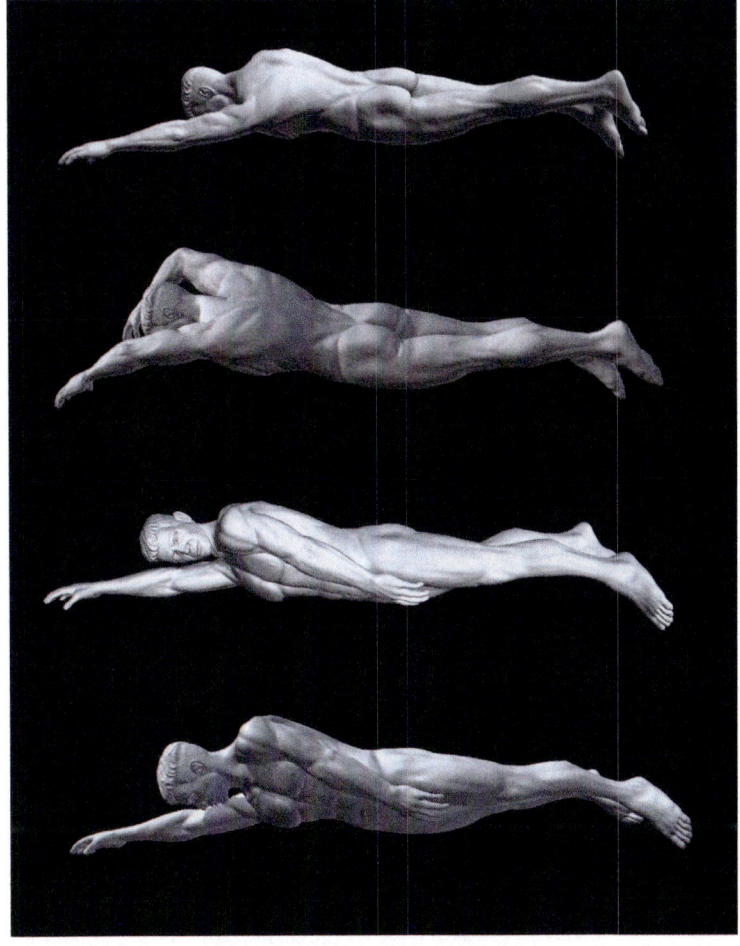

Figure 9.6: Interrupted breath.

to continue swimming and tries to perform the next arm recovery. So it may take a few practices before you are able to stop with one arm in the *Streamline* position, the other forearm just inside the hip bone, and just glide for a second or two before standing up.

This is a fantastic way to rehearse the position we need to be in before, during, and after the breath in order to maintain stability. Once you've practised this several times on one side, do the same thing on the other side. At this point, it is interesting to notice how each side feels. Does one side feel more familiar or easier? Does one side feel impossible to get right? These are excellent mental notes to help you with your practice. It is also interesting to note that, often, what feels most comfortable when working on breathing is not always correct. Frequently, survival instinct takes over and puts us into exaggerated positions to be absolutely sure that we get air. It takes a lot of discipline to work just outside of your comfort zone in order to overcome this natural tendency.

9.1.2 Body position

You are now going to repeat the above exercise and simply change the cue. This time, you're going to focus on body position. Once again, you will start off in your *Build the Frame with Arms* position, take two slow, controlled non-breathing strokes, and, on the 3rd stroke, focus on looking directly next to you as you allow the head to rotate around with the whole body. Each time you practise this, mentally note what you can see in your surroundings. If you are in a swimming pool, you want to look no higher than the edge of the pool. You could look at a grout line or a rail, just something that you can focus on so you can build up an awareness of whether your turned head is staying neutral or whether you are looking at something behind you, which would break your head-spine alignment. Because you are only doing this with one stroke at the moment, you can find a specific point in the pool as a visual aid. Obviously, this becomes more challenging when you add in more strokes and continue up the length of the pool, and that is why it is essential to build up an awareness of the sensation you feel when you are doing it correctly through repetition of just a few strokes. Again, practise this equally on both sides.

Next, repeat the same practice pattern, and this time take your focus to sending the *Cuckoo* hand to the *Streamline* position. On the 3rd stroke, allow the weight shift to send the fingernails of the Cuckoo arm forwards, or to the front wall of the pool, still allowing the head to turn with the rotation. You are simply changing the focus.

9.1.3 Air management

As you push off you will begin a slow release of bubbles out through the nose. Then, on the stroke where you are going to integrate the breath, begin your more exaggerated exhalation through the nose. At the same instant, you begin to allow the head to move round towards the air with the rotation. This exhalation should last until your mouth is just about to break through the surface of the water, at which point you can release your diaphragm, and allow the inhalation to happen. As soon as you return your face into the water, repeat this cycle.

9.1.4 Return head

As soon as your mouth has cleared the surface and you have allowed the diaphragmatic inhalation to happen, simply release your head, turning it back to a face-down, neutral position.

The sequence is a simultaneous, whole-body movement to the breath, followed by a head return that is independent of the rest of the stroke. (see Figure 9.7)

Figure 9.7: Whole Stroke Integrated Breathing sequence.

Summary of Cues: Integrated breathing

- » Rotate head with whole body at the moment of weight shift
- » Look directly next to you
- » Weight shift: send fingernails to streamline position
- » Exhale explosively as head rotates to the air
- » Release head to neutral as soon as the inhalation has happened

Chapter 10

Catch

Are you one of the readers who skipped straight to this chapter? If so, as tempting as it is to continue reading on from here, I would highly recommend taking the time to read through, and practise, the exercises in all the previous chapters, as this will give you the foundation to enable you to physically be able to perform the *Catch* correctly and safely.

There are two questions that are most often asked by new clients coming to my studio, workshops or open water camps: one concerns the breathing sequence, and the other, the *Catch*. People say that they can swim quite well, but they would just love to know how to do the '*Catch*' thing. Many first sessions with my clients are interspersed with questions about the *Catch*. I never answer these questions in the first session, which is often frustrating for the client, but it is certainly in their best interests. Focusing on more than one new thing at a time is physically impossible. If the brain focuses on *Catch* in those early stages, our focus will be on the arms, which are, more often than not, disconnected, and this will reinforce our terrestrial mammalian instinct to pull. We must first *Build the Frame*, connecting the legs to the torso, to ensure a stable platform upon which to add every other movement. The disconnected arms make it impossible to achieve the correct position of the *Catch* arm anatomically, but even more importantly, it is impossible to achieve the correct timing of the *Catch*. The synchronisation of the *Catch* being correct or not will determine which muscle groups you are able to use to carry out this action, and whether you are able to hold on to the water rather than just slipping through it and trying to pull it behind you. In my opinion, most swimming-induced shoulder injuries are associated with incorrect *Catch* mechanics. For example, often a *Catch* goes too wide because the arm is not in the correct starting position, so simply trying to make the *Catch* narrower won't fix the problem. The width of the Catch can be a cause of shoulder injury, but it is not always the root cause, as I will now explain.

Finding the root cause

Here is an example to explain what I mean. A common mistake that traditional coaches pick up on is their swimmers arms crossing their centre line as they swim, causing them to snake their way down the pool or across a lake. The corrective instruction that the swimmer is then always given when this error is detected is to aim to swim pointing the hands at 10 to 2 on a clock face. This is a purposeful exaggeration rather than the intended outcome, and can appear to remedy the problem in the short term. The swimmer sets off with this in mind and perfectly executes a much straighter line in the pool by sending their hands towards what they believe to be 10 o'clock and 2 o'clock. While they are absolutely focused on going to these perceived positions, they achieve them. However, as soon as their focus strays or turns to something else, the swimmer reverts to crossing the centre line and snaking their way down the pool as before. The reason that a swimmer will revert to exhibiting the original problem, snaking, is because the instigating movement that is causing the swimmer to go across the centre line is actually happening much earlier in the stroke, and unless that instigator is changed, the problem of crossing the centre line will always come back as soon as the swimmer is not focused on the 'quick fix' instruction.

This principle applies in all areas of our lives. As human beings, we are really good at focusing on the problem at hand and trying to fix that, but not so successful at delving deeper, at finding out what the actual root cause of the problem is, so that we can stop it from ever happening again. This is why improvement projects in work settings use root cause analysis tools, such as the Five Whys or Fishbone diagrams, to make sure they correctly identify the real issue and don't start prematurely looking for solutions to what they thought was the problem. The same approach is needed when trying to learn new movement patterns in the body, too. It is irrelevant which sport or activity you are involved in, the principle remains the same. When learning the *Catch*, keeping this principle at the forefront of your mind will ensure you reach your goal faster. A poorly shaped or timed *Catch* will always be because of one of 3 things: a poor arm recovery, entry or extension point. The human body is an amazing vessel, and if you put yours into the correct position to begin with, then everything that follows can also be correct.

Early vertical forearm

The early vertical forearm, or EVF, as it is known in the swimming world, is something that many swimmers strive to achieve. So what is it? As you can see in Figure 10.1 below, it is literally what it says on the tin: it is having the forearm vertical as early in the stroke as possible. When you pause Olympic freestylers in action, or watch them in slow motion, you can often see great examples of what people call an early vertical forearm. However, there are a few things that must be taken into consideration when trying to emulate Olympians and other elite swimmers.

Figure 10.1: Example of Early Vertical Forearm (Source: Openwaterpedia).

The first thing to remember is the Olympic and elite swimming world is probably made up of about 2% of the swimming population, if that. Therefore, 98% of the swimming population are non-elite swimmers. It is important to realise the perspective and timing of the much sought after EVF: the forearm should be vertical once the swimmer is halfway through their rotation, and this is often what we see the Olympians doing. Sometimes it can appear that the elbow is bent at a 90-degree angle before the swimmer has rotated but it is often actually the angle of the swimmer in relation to the camera. This is often misunderstood as the perspective is not taken into account.

Secondly, Olympic swimmers are commonly of a certain age group and have probably had competing in the Olympics in their sights for as long as they can remember. They are typically younger, so have many factors on their side, most importantly flexibility, giving them greater range of movement.

Thirdly, when we look at Olympians we often see anomalies, such as certain body types: longer than usual wingspans, very long feet, ratios between torso length and legs that benefit a particular stroke, hypermobility that allows the swimmer to practically dislocate the shoulder joint with ease or flex their backs more than normal, et cetera. This is just a short list of some of the anomalies I've seen over the years when studying Olympic swimmers.

And lastly, Olympic swimmers have spent huge amounts of time on training, practice and stroke work to become the incredible swimmers they are. They have put in many hours every week practising in the swimming pool. Most of us non-elite swimmers are able to get to the pool for an hour or two, perhaps three, or a maximum of four, times a week.

Because we are not in the 2% of the elite swimmer population, without the talents and anomalies Olympians are born with, or their extensive training regimes, we have to rely heavily on learning technique because it does not come naturally to the rest of the us. And when it comes to thinking about the *Catch*, it has to be less about aesthetics and trying to make shapes, and more about connecting the body up correctly, so that these shapes become by-products of correct joint mechanics. This way, we can be more confident that our movement patterns will remain effective, safe, strong and well-timed.

'Pull': a swear word in my book

Commonly, swim sets are heavily focussed on 'pull', using a variety of pool toys to 'help' swimmers train the 'pull'. These sets are often metabolically challenging and the swimmer is likely to get out of the pool with a stroke that has deteriorated rather than improved, because the focus has been on 'pulling' as hard as possible, with and without aids, in an attempt to haul the body as quickly as possible through the water. The intended outcome of this type of set is to strengthen the shoulder muscles. However, this can only work if the swimmer is using the correct groups of larger muscles at the right time. Otherwise, the swimmer is just overloading individual smaller muscles around the shoulder joint, which is the most inherently unstable joint in the human body, potentially leading to shoulder injury.

As we have previously discussed, even the words we use can be very powerful and can result in incorrect movements being made.

Let's talk more about 'pulling'. The use of this word - or not - is key to transforming how your brain thinks swimming should work. First, I want to demonstrate what happens physically in your body when you think of, or try to execute, the action of 'pull'. Our brains develop connections between sensations and words, connotations if you will, and once we understand the power of these connotations, we can change the words we use to encourage a correct action or movement.

Dryland exploration

» Walk up to a door. Hold onto the handle with one hand, and pull the door towards you.
» Repeat this action, and notice what happens to your elbow.
» Did you notice that your elbow drops downwards and towards your rib cage as you perform the word "pull" the door? (See Figure 10.2a)
» Now go to the edge of a kitchen counter, or a dining table, and hold onto the end of this table or counter by pressing with the inside of your wrist to help move your body towards your hand. (See Figure 10.2b) Again, pay particular attention to what your elbow does whilst you are executing this exercise.
» What you should notice is that, as you apply pressure to the end of the counter in order to send your body

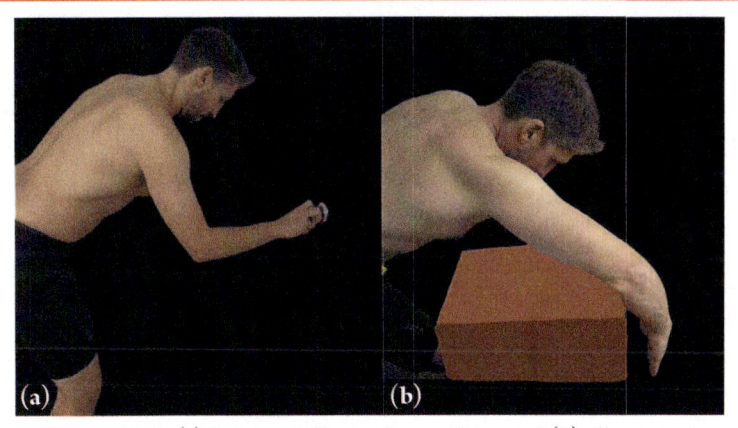

Figure 10.2: (a) Dropped elbow when pulling, and (b) elbow staying forward when holding.

forwards, your elbow will actually bend up and outwards to create a lever.

This second illustration explains the exact movement that we want to let happen with our *Catch*. Note the use of the word let happen, rather than make happen. As soon as we use the word 'pull', our elbow will drop, and we will be unable to 'hold on to' the water with the catching arm. This might lead you to think that, if you should not drop your elbow, then you must keep your elbow up, and create an early vertical forearm that way, but that would just be another example of trying to fix the apparent problem, rather than identifying and tackling the cause. Yes, thinking of keeping the elbow up during the *Catch* will, no doubt, work to some extent, but if the arm is not in the correct position to begin with, as soon as you let go of the focus, the elbow will instantly drop again. We want to ensure the arm is in the correct position so that it folds into a *Catch* shape naturally. When the *Catch* is performed correctly, the elbow gives the impression of being high, but this is just a matter of perspective. In actual fact, the elbow height has simply been maintained, not raised.

Shape

The shape of the *Catch* should happen as a by-product of the correct *Streamline* setup and synchronisation point. However, let's take a moment to explore what shape we are aiming for. The start of the *Catch* happens at the moment the swimmer hits their *Streamline* position, the point where the whole body, including the scapula, has sent the fingernails to the front wall of the pool. As we already know from Chapter 6 Streamline, the arm is attached to the body via the scapula, and is engaged but not tense. We continue this engaged feeling as the elbow begins to fold, almost as if the arm is trying to shape itself over a large gym ball, making a soft hook shape (see Figure 10.3). The upper arm stays in place, giving the impression of the elbow being high. This shape is created by moving the elbow joint, not by bending at the wrist. The wrist should remain straight during most parts of the *Catch* phase. A common error with people working on their *Catch* is that they create the *Catch* shape with their wrists, which results in pressure being applied in the wrong direction, a dropped elbow, and the potential for shoulder injury.

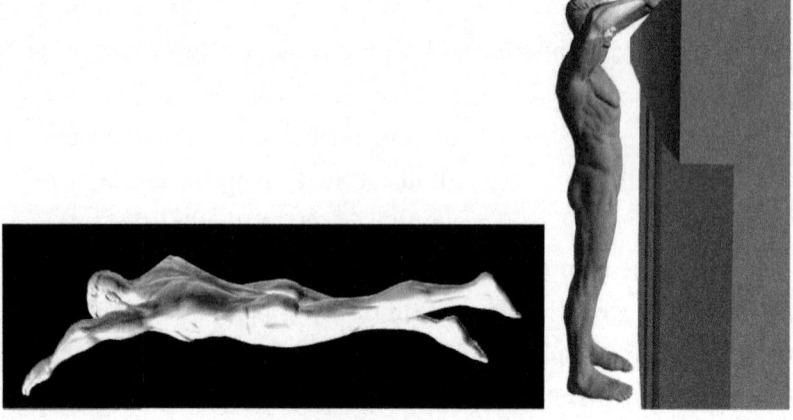

Figure 10.3: Catch Shape.

Dryland activity 10.1

10.1.1 Fold at the elbow with both arms

Standing upright with feet hip-width apart in your Build the Frame with Arms position, ensure that your scapulae have sent your fingernails towards the ceiling above you. Fold at both elbows as if you are going to place your forearms and hands on the top of a high wall in front of you (see Figure 10.4). Once you are in the correct position, your hands will still be higher than your head. Ensure that your frame remains in place as you fold your elbows, and that the palms of your hands are facing the floor.

Figure 10.4: Folding both arms at the elbow.

10.1.2 Fold at the elbow in streamline

This particular rehearsal is most beneficial when performed in front of a mirror. Stand in your, now well-rehearsed, vertical *Streamline* position. Once you are sure you're in the correct position, use your scapula to slide your fingernails to the ceiling, then, maintaining this position, just allow the arm to fold at the elbow. (See Figure 10.5) Ensure that, as you slide the scapula towards the ceiling and fold at the elbow, you do not compromise your frame at all, paying particular attention to your head to feet line. There should be no movement happening anywhere in the rest of your body; it should stay completely still. You should feel engaged - but not stretched. Practise this several times on each side.

Figure 10.5:

It is also possible to practise this in your lunge position, where it can be helpful to get a sense of how this feels when horizontal. However, it is impossible to mimic the true horizontal sensation on land, as we cannot levitate. Getting into the lunge position helps us feel as close as possible to the sensation we get in the water, but do be mindful that it will feel different to when we are in the pool, because we are bent at the hips in the lunge position, and, obviously, in the water we are straight. I do not recommend trying the standing rehearsal in the lunge position if you have any back, hip or knee pain.

Get into the lunge position you used when practising the arm recovery, but, this time, lengthen the *Streamline* arm out in front, rather than resting it on your knee. Once again, you are going to use the scapula to send the fingernails forwards towards the wall in front of you, and, maintaining this position, fold at the elbow. Practise this on both sides (see Figure 10.6). It is important to ensure that, when folding at the elbow, your focus is on allowing the forearm to move by bending the elbow joint only; if the upper arm has remained connected to the torso through the scapula, it will move correctly, and only very slightly, in response.

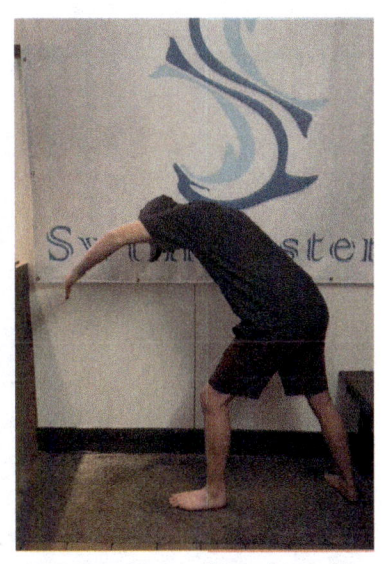

Figure 10.6: Standing rehearsal in lunge position showing *Catch* fold.

Pool activity 10.1

10.1.1 Fold at the elbow with both arms

The first thing to do is push off in the *Build the Frame with Arms* position (see Figure 10.7a). Remind yourself to maintain the frame and to use the scapulae to send the fingernails to the other end of the pool. Then fold at both elbows, whilst maintaining the scapula position. It is helpful, at this point, to imagine you are folding your arms over a swiss ball that is just in front of you (see Figure 10.7b). Then apply pressure to the

The SwimMastery Way

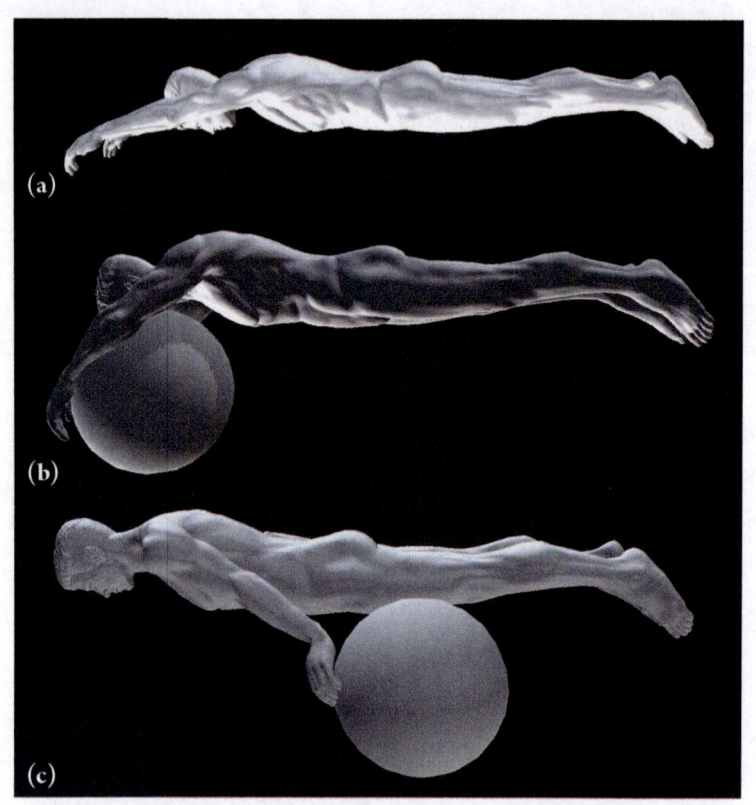

Figure 10.7: (a) *Build The Frame with Arms*, (b) *Build The Frame with Arms* fold over ball, and (c) *Build The Frame with Arms* send body past the ball.

forearms, hands and wrists, ensuring that you are pressing the swiss ball consistently towards the back wall of the pool (see Figure 10.7c). Then simultaneously, using the pressure created, send the Middle Trident (the top of the head) towards the wall in front of you. (see Figure 10.7c) As you create pressure and send the head forwards, it is imperative that you maintain your frame. A useful cue to use during this exercise is to imagine that, as you apply pressure, you are sending your head further away from your feet, which helps you to maintain the middle Trident prong.

When first performing this exercise, some common errors you may make are to push the head down and send yourself down towards the bottom of the pool, or to collapse at the hips and not maintain the frame. The idea is to apply pressure to the arms and transfer that pressure directly into forward momentum through the top of the head, a bit like a torpedo or an arrow. As you repeat this exercise you will find that the water may start to feel slightly 'thicker' as you are able to, literally, hold onto it, as if applying pressure to a solid object and sending the head forwards. This exercise is an excellent way to learn to feel the water and to make the most of transferring pressure into forward momentum.

10.1.2 Fold at the elbow in streamline

Practise the dryland rehearsal (10.1.2) several times with each arm before setting off in the water, to remind your body of the sensation. Then push off in your *Build the Frame with Arms* position, move into your *Streamline* position, and simply use the scapula to send the fingernails to the far end of the pool. This will be a good reminder to your body of the correct *Streamline* position, remembering that the *Streamline* position is made up of the whole body from the fingernails (not fingertips) all the way to the feet. Practise this exercise several times on each side before moving on to the next step. Flutter your legs during these exercises, (but please note this is not a kicking drill), and each repeat should last only as long as one comfortable breath.

Next, push off in your correct *Streamline* position and simply practise folding at the elbow and folding over your swiss ball, remembering that the shape is a soft hook and that

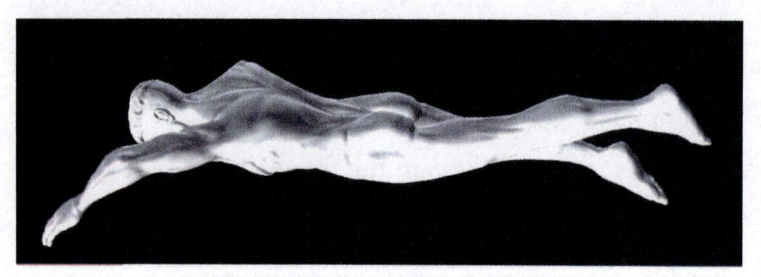

Figure 10.8: Streamline fold (soft hook).

you are not bending the arm to vertical (see Figure 10.8). Then straighten the arm back to *Streamline* and repeat. Then repeat the above, starting with *Build the Frame with Arms*, this time going to *Streamline* on the other side.

10.1.3 Practise the shape in whole stroke

Next, you are going to put this into the whole stroke. Push off in your *Build the Frame with Arms* position, move into your *Streamline* position, and, as you take each stroke, simply use the scapula to send the fingernails to the far end of the pool, and then fold at the elbow. Do this for six strokes without taking a breath and then stand up. Please note that, at this point, you are simply practising the position and the shape; you are not looking to apply any pressure to the water at this

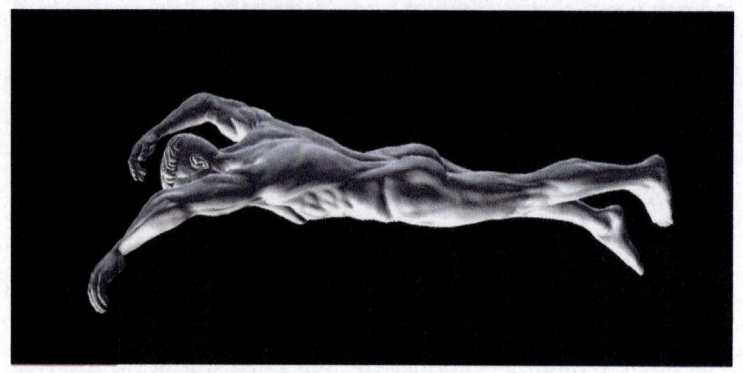

Figure 10.9: Whole stroke fold (soft hook).

> stage. Keep practising until you are sure that when you fold at the elbow the upper arm is not immediately dropping, but note that you are not trying to hold the upper arm up, as this will cause shoulder injury. You are just ensuring that the scapula is still sending the upper arm forward while folding at the elbow (see Figure 10.9).

Anchoring

The *Catch* functions primarily to make contact with, and hold onto, the water, almost as if it's an anchor, so the body can rotate and lengthen past that point. We are not trying to pull the water that is in front of us, behind us. We are, in fact, keeping that water still, holding onto it, and moving the body past it. This is a difficult concept for some swimmers to grasp, as we are hard wired to 'pull' - and to think 'pull' - as if we were trying to use our arms and hands as paddles to haul the body through the water. Take a moment to consider kayaking or rowing; you will notice that when the rower places the paddle in the water and applies pressure, the paddle actually stays in more or less the same place it entered the water, while the boat, along with the rower, moves past it. The rower then has to remove the paddle from where they first placed it in the water, and move it to the next point of entry, ready to 'hold' that water for the next stroke (see Figure 10.10). Because we are

Figure 10.10: Rower sequence.

swimming in water, just as a rower is rowing in water, the same principle must surely apply?

Catch Pathway

What the pathway of the *Catch* should be is always an interesting and much-debated issue. The most important consideration when thinking about the pathway is how we can perform it and keep the joints safe and injury-free. The second priority to consider is the direction in which we apply the pressure. As mentioned earlier, Newton discovered that for every action there is an equal and opposite reaction. Therefore, we are going to move in the opposite direction to the direction in which we apply pressure. That is a rule of physics.

If we extend our arm so far out in front as to perceivably make ourselves more streamlined, but have the arm so high that the hand is just beneath the surface of the water, then we are going to turn that lever into a long, weak one, which will result in the next movement being the arm falling away in a downwards direction. Applying pressure downwards in this manner is going to result in the rest of the body going upwards, creating a bouncy stroke that is very commonly seen in public pools around the world.

Swimmers often follow another common principle that, in order to get the maximum amount of propulsion in water, you need to increase the distance that your hand travels during the catch, sadly disregarding the direction it travels in. So swimmers are encouraged to sweep outwards, and then inwards, and then back, and then up, to create this long pathway, sometimes known as the 'S' shaped pull. However, when we remind ourselves of Newton's third law of motion (above), by sweeping outwards and inwards, then back up, physics tells us that we will move the body in the opposite directions in response. This will create a snaking-type stroke (see Figure 10.11)

Figure 10.11: Incorrect catch pathway.

So, how do we take advantage of Newton's Law? Well, logically, in order to go forwards we can only apply pressure backwards. We also know that it is impossible to hold on to moving water. Therefore, to create the most efficient and safe *Catch* pathway, we first need to ensure that the water around the hand and back of the forearm is still, and secondly ensure that, during the entire *Catch*, the palm of the hand and the inside of the forearm are only ever facing directly behind the swimmer. Bearing all this in mind, the *Catch* pathway can only be straight. If I want to move my body in a straight line forwards, I need to apply pressure in a straight line backwards.

In order to understand how this is achieved, we need to take perspective into account. A straight *Catch* pathway can give an observer who is only focusing attention on the hand, the illusion that the hand is sweeping in, out, back and up. But it is just that - an illusion, created by focussing on the hand in isolation, and not the hand in relation to the whole-body rotation. When focusing on the hand in relation to the actual body of the swimmer, who is performing a correct and safe *Catch* pathway, it is very clear to see that it is actually moving in a straight line. As we fold the elbow from the *Streamline* position, because of how the joints react, the hand must not stay in line with the shoulder, as it was in *Streamline*. If it was to stay in line with the shoulder, this would stop you swimming

The SwimMastery Way

in a straight line, would compromise the shoulder joint and would likely cause injury. When the fold at the elbow has been executed correctly, the hand will fall just inside of that line and the elbow will actually fall just outside of that line (see Figure 10.12a). Therefore, the *Catch* pathway is a straight line that begins just inside the *Streamline* line and ends in our *Build the Frame with No Arms* arm position, i.e. with the inside of the elbow resting on the front of the rib cage and the forearm just inside the front hip bone (see Figure 10.12b).

Figure 10.12: (a) Hand inside elbow outside, and (b) correct catch pathway.

Talking about the *Catch* pathway is a very tricky subject, and one I don't talk about very often at all. The reason for this is that the most important part of the *Catch* is the part that happens forward of the head and shoulders. At the moment that we have begun to apply pressure as a result of the weight shift, we really want the swimmer's focus to be on channelling the energy created into forward momentum through the middle Trident prong and the *Streamline* arm on the other side. If I talk to the swimmer about the last part of the *Catch* pathway, unfortunately that is where their focus is going to be. This focus can result in dead spots and deceleration in the stroke.

However, it is sometimes necessary to talk about it, as swimmers can make either one of two errors. Some swimmers stop their *Catch* far too early and, as a result, lose out on some very important anchoring time, resulting in less distance travelled per stroke. Others carry their *Catch* pathway on for too long, and finish by pushing upwards past the hip, which results in two problems. Firstly, as already discussed, pushing water upwards will send the swimmer downwards. More importantly, pushing water upwards will force the arm and the scapula into a compromised position, from which the swimmer is unable to recover safely or efficiently. This can lead to injury.

So, where does the *Catch* finish? As we have already pointed out, the *Catch* finishes in the *Build the Frame without Arms* position. It finishes with a straight arm. Once the body has started to move forwards past the arm, the swimmer must continue to apply pressure directly behind them until the arm is straight, at which point they need to release that arm and send the scapula out wide and forwards to perform the next part of the stroke, which is the arm recovery. This results in a stroke that can take advantage of maximum anchoring and travelling distance, while staying fluid and ensuring the body stays in a position that allows it to perform the next arm recovery safely.

Pressure

In previous chapters we have spent time on *Building the Frame*, learning the correct *Streamline* position, thinking about how the arm *recovers* above the water, talking about the *Synchronisation* points of the stroke and our *Integrated Breathing* positions and timing. Now these are all in place, we can look at maintaining each one of those positions and connected body parts as we start to introduce the idea of propulsion with the *Catch*.

Once the shape practice, above, becomes familiar, and you can execute it with ease, you can move on to thinking about water pressure. There are many places where we feel the pressure of the water; for example, previously I have discussed feeling water pressure on your face when finding the correct head position. Being able to tune in to the pressure of the water on your arm will vastly aid your ability to learn to hold it. The more you tune in, the more thick the water will begin to feel.

When we begin to think about applying pressure, we need to link it to Newton's Third Law of Motion: for every action, there is an equal and opposite reaction. We are always going to move in the opposite direction to that in which we have applied the pressure. It is obvious that, as a swimmer, we always want to go forwards and therefore it should be equally obvious that the only direction we ever want to apply pressure in, is backwards.

Once you've applied pressure in the first part of the catch, your focus then needs to shift to the recovering arm on the other side. So long as you are applying pressure towards the back wall of the pool for the entire *Catch* phase, your arm will always end up in the right place.

As typical human swimmers, the instinct is very strong to pull and kick, as we have explained previously. The key to success in learning an effective and safe swim technique is teaching the nervous system that it is the weight shift of the whole body rotation that begins the process of forward propulsion, and this is what allows us to start applying pressure effectively and safely. I often use the analogy of an outboard motor of a boat: it has both an engine and a propeller. These two elements work in unison to create both the power and the forward momentum, but neither one will make the boat go forwards on its own. It is the same with swimming: we have the weight shift, with the whole-body rotation being equivalent to the engine, and the limbs, being equivalent to the propeller. Moving the limbs in isolation of the rotation is not effective and is very tiring. Similarly, having the whole body rotation without the limbs anchoring on the water is also ineffective and creates little propulsion. Up to this point we have built both elements separately, but now the time has come to integrate them to send the body forwards.

Pool activity 10.2

10.2.1 Feel pressure

Begin by swimming several 25s, just tuning into different parts of your body and seeing where you are currently feeling pressure, if anywhere. Swim the next length experiencing what you feel on your fingernails as you are swimming. On the next repeat, tune in to whether you can feel any pressure on the inside of the forearm. On the third repeat, tune into your head and your face and see if you can feel any pressure on the top of your head, or along your face, as you swim. You will now have discovered where you do and do not feel pressure; make a mental note of this.

Pool activity 10.3

10.3.1 Feel pressure on fingernails and forearm

Take 4 to 6 non-breathing strokes focusing on rotating forwards into your Streamline position. Notice what you feel on the fingernails. You may need to practise this several times before you can actually feel anything. The more you are able to tune in and focus on this area of the body, the more you should be able to feel slight pressure against the fingernails, almost as if the water is tickling them (see Figure 10.13). Then add breathing, and notice what changes you feel in the pressure on the fingernails during the breath. Does anything change? If it does, this suggests that you need to revisit your *Streamline* position and your *Integrated breathing* position, focusing particularly on the timing, as well as hitting and maintaining that *Streamline* position during the breath. Practise this until the sensation of pressure on your fingernails doesn't change, whether you are breathing or not breathing.

Figure 10.13: Feel pressure on the fingernails.

We will now add the fold. On the next 6 strokes, as soon as you feel the pressure on your fingernails, fold at the elbow. If you have executed this correctly, you should now feel pressure on the inside of the forearm (see Figure 10.14). The idea here is to feel pressure on the fingernails, fold at the elbow, and transfer the feeling of pressure from the fingernails to the inside of the forearm. Watch out for a common issue, at this point, which is that as soon as we try to fold at the elbow, it can collapse and drop downwards, rather than remaining forward, creating one of the main problems found in the traditional *Catch* pathway, as discussed before (see Figure 10.15). If your

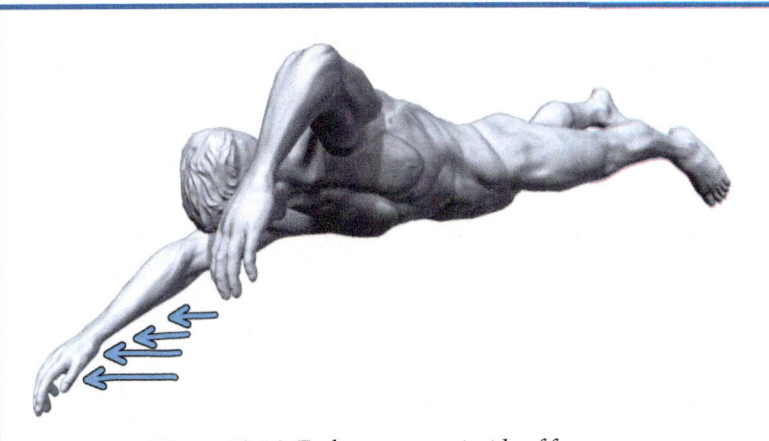

Figure 10.14: Feel pressure on inside of forearm.

Figure 10.15: Dropped elbow catch.

elbow drops, you will not feel any pressure on the inside of your forearm, so this sensation of pressure is an excellent cue. I recommend practising the fold in isolation in your streamline position to remind your nervous system of the movement. Even though you are working in whole stroke, it is sometimes necessary to focus on one arm at a time during this exercise. For example, do a few repeats just sending your focus to your left arm, feeling the pressure as you send the body into the streamline position, and maintaining the sensation of pressure as you fold at the elbow. Then repeat the same exercise, only focusing on the right arm.

I ask people to imagine that they are swimming over a ladder that is lying about a foot underneath them. I suggest they imagine that, with each stroke, they are sending their

The SwimMastery Way

body along the ladder in the Streamline position, and then simply hooking the forearm over the next rung of the ladder. They can then apply pressure to this rung on the next weight shift, which sends the body forwards into the next *Streamline* position (see Figure 10.16).

Figure 10.16: Catch on ladder.

This will also help to remind yourself of which direction you are applying pressure in as your body moves forward past the rung of the ladder, or 'held' water. Swim a few repeats, again without breathing to begin with, focussing - at that moment of weight shift - on applying pressure directly behind you, in order to send the body forwards. If your Streamline position is compromised in any way at all, it will result in you applying pressure in the wrong direction, which, in turn, can cause injury in the shoulder joint. Spending time on your frame and your *Streamline* position will put your body into the best possible position to be able to apply pressure in the right direction (see Figure 10.17).

10.3.2 Keep the water still

The next cue that I recommend is to hook the arm over the rung of the imaginary ladder and think about keeping that

Catch

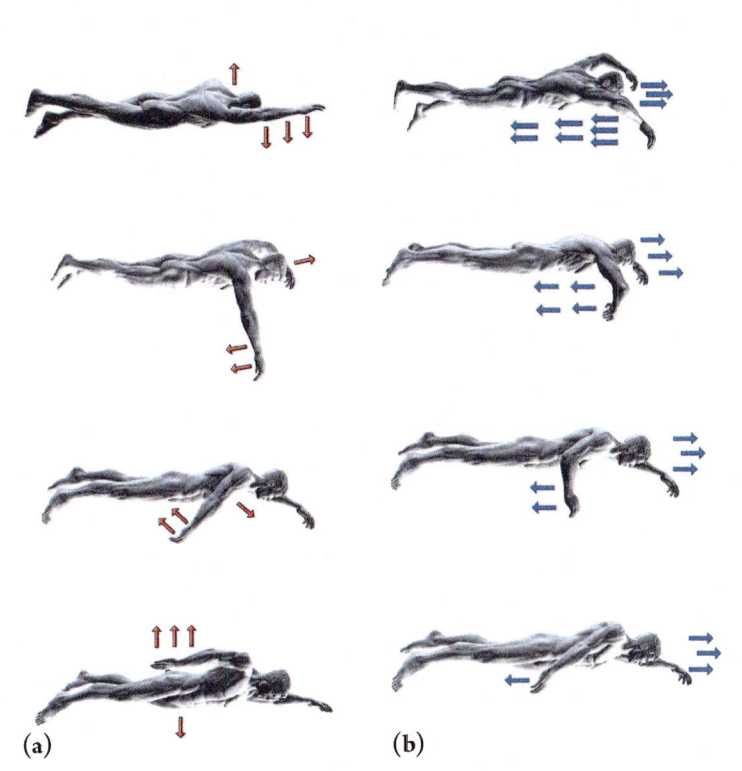

Figure 10.17: (a) Incorrect catch pathway, and (b) correct catch pathway.

hand and forearm completely still as you rotate and send the body forwards. Imagine you are trying to keep the water around your forearm as still as you possibly can during this phase of each stroke. It is very tempting to apply too much pressure and end up just moving, or throwing, water down the pool behind you, rather than having the sense of holding onto the water and using it as an anchor to send the body past.

10.3.3 Apply different amounts of pressure

The last process to practise is applying and maintaining different amounts of pressure to the water as you shift weight and rotate past it. For example, on the first repeat, see how lightly you can 'hold on to the rung of the ladder' whilst rotating past it, and then gradually, with each repeat, increase the amount of pressure that you are applying to the rung of the ladder, and notice what happens to your rate of forward momentum. As you become more body aware and more sensitive to the feeling of the water, you will find that you are able to apply three or, maybe, four different degrees of pressure that transfer into forward momentum. Too little pressure and the body won't go anywhere. The same is true of too much pressure as, when we apply too much pressure we move the water, our hand slips and is unable to hold on to the anchor, and therefore the body cannot move past it. At both ends of this spectrum of applied pressure, it can feel effortful.

Summary of cues: Catch

- » Feel the pressure on your fingernails
- » Fold at the elbow
- » Maintain a forward scapula
- » Use the weight shift to send the body past the anchor
- » Send energy forward through the Middle Trident
- » Feel the transfer of pressure from fingernails to inside of forearm as you fold
- » Apply different amounts of pressure
- » Synchronise pressure with weight-shift

Chapter 11

Two-beat leg press

When teaching swimmers about the correct two-beat leg mechanics, I remove the word 'kick'. As I explained in Chapter 5: Flutter, there is a common association and response to this word. But there is another reason for not using this word. When you are next in the swimming pool, stand and, using your quads and hamstrings, draw back your heel by bending the knee and kick it forward, as if to kick a football. Notice what you feel against the front of your shin and the front of your foot. Also, tune into what the water does. You should notice that it moves around a lot and may even create bubbles. Now repeat Pool activity 5.1.1 from Chapter 5: Flutter, standing on a brick or step in the water; draw the back of the thigh behind the body line and then sweep the front of the thigh forward. Notice how different the water feels against your leg. How do the sensations differ on your shin and the front of your foot? Could it be that the water feels slightly thicker? A bit more like treacle, perhaps? Do you notice how much stiller the water is? Repeat this several times to get a good feel for the difference between the sensation of kicking and the sensation of the second movement, which is more of a press. As we touched on in Chapter 10: Catch, it is impossible to hold onto moving water, and if we cannot hold on to moving water, we cannot use it as an anchor to press against to aid rotation and send the body forwards. This is where the legs become important in swimming freestyle, as explained in Chapter 5.

Your legs are the anchor point around which the whole body can rotate. A good way to illustrate this concept is to sit on an office or swivel chair. Take your feet off the floor and try to rotate yourself in the chair. This will be very difficult to do; you will find that the legs go in one direction, and the upper body and arms go in the other direction, as your body tries to create some form of swivelling action. Now, plant your feet on the floor and rotate yourself. This now becomes easy. When you do this, notice that you are not necessarily using your feet to push yourself around, but using them as an anchor as you swivel the whole body around. The two-beat leg press in swimming gives us that same anchoring function, while also helping to control the amount of whole-body rotation. This anchoring function of the legs also allows the body to stop swivelling at a certain point, so you can control the *Streamline* position and direct your energy forwards.

The legs can also provide a small amount of propulsion. Much like a propeller, or corkscrew, the whole body rotates while the legs apply pressure to the water. Imagine they are directing this force behind you in order to send the head, the top of the corkscrew or middle trident, forwards.

> ### Pool activity 11.1 Maintaining Whole Body Connection and Preparing for a Two-Beat Leg Press
>
> We need to explore and discover what our legs are doing at present so that we can make changes in the right way. Having worked through the earlier chapters and developing your proprioception, you are now more aware of your body and will be better able to feel what your legs are doing.

Start by pushing off into your stable platform (*Build the Frame with Arms* position), ensuring that you are well connected, all the way from head to feet. By now, this should feel familiar and easy to achieve. If not, I would suggest spending more practice time on those connections before attempting this next section. Once you've pushed off in your connected position, take six strokes, focusing on rotating your whole body and lengthening through the head. Imagine that your legs are an extension of your torso, and, therefore, part of the rotation. What did you feel? What did your legs do? The results during this practice will, of course, vary between swimmers.

After exploring what happens to your legs when you swim, you will have a clear indication of how they tend to respond and move. This is the first step towards being able to make any changes. Each individual will be at a different stage and will experience varying amounts of disruption or control over their legs. Nevertheless, I recommend that everyone works through each of the next steps, albeit some may be able to progress through the steps faster than others.

Counterbalance

The first thing we want to do is to imprint the *Counterbalance* position. Let's understand it theoretically first. When you are in the left *Streamline* position, you will be rotated on your 3 points of contact which you first learned in Chapter 6: Streamline. To put the body into the *Counterbalance* position do a very small 'scissor' with the legs, by drawing the left thigh slightly behind the body and having the right thigh slightly in front of the body. Picture yourself lying in a tube with a diameter no wider than the width of your

The SwimMastery Way

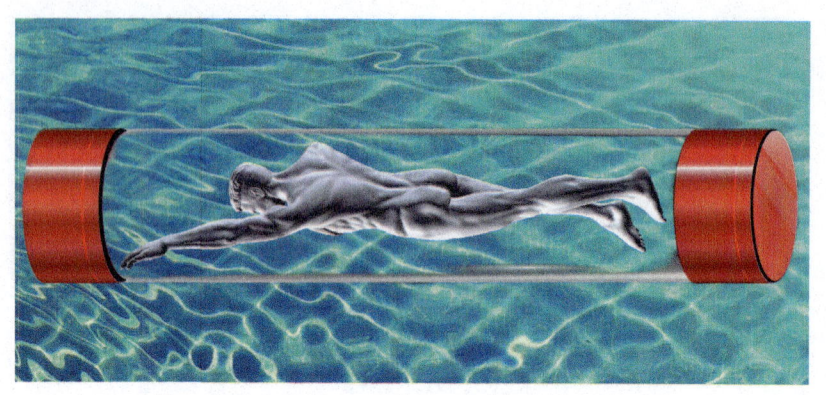

Figure 11.1: Swimming through the width of a tube.

shoulders all the way around: your legs, forward and backward, should be no wider than the diameter of the tube. (See Figure 11.1).

An important point to note is the direction in which you draw the thigh backwards and send the thigh forwards. In relation to your body, you are simply drawing the thigh behind you and sending the thigh in front of you, exactly as you would do in walking. In the swimming pool, you are drawing the thigh back at the same angle as your rotation, i.e., sending the front thigh towards the same place that your belly button is pointing, and the back thigh in the opposite direction. I find that when swimmers understand this, it actually helps them to stay connected, because, until then, they often, subconsciously, try to move their legs straight up and down, not taking the rotation into consideration. This causes the body to become disconnected. Realising that our legs move in the same direction as the torso eliminates this disconnection.

Dryland Activity 11.1 Standing rehearsal

11.1.1 Feel the position

Stand up, preferably in front of a mirror, with your legs within your hips, so your feet are no wider than hip-distance apart and your legs are not squeezed together. Set your frame: touch your head to the ceiling, and move your pelvis into the correct position so that you can feel all the core muscle engagement, as you have learnt previously. Now, swivelling on the balls of your feet, rotate your 8 laser beams to the left corner of the room, ensuring your head remains in its neutral position, then lower your heels. This will result in your legs being slightly apart, with one leg behind the bodyline and one leg in front of the bodyline, with your weight distributed evenly on both feet (see Figure 11.2a). Next, raise your right arm and, using your scapula, slide the arm and fingernails up to the ceiling: this is your Counterbalance body position (see Figure 11.2b).

Now repeat the same exercise, but on the other side. Starting with your feet next to each other (ankles under hip joint), rotate your 8 laser beams to the right corner of the room, ensuring your head remains in its neutral position.

Figure 11.2: (a) Feel the position: Step 1, and (b) Feel the position: Step 2 Counterbalance.

Then raise the left arm and use the scapula to slide the arm and fingernails to the ceiling.

11.1.2 Feel the movement

For this exercise, it is advantageous to have a slightly slippery surface to stand on, for example, wearing socks on a bathroom floor.

Stand up and create your frame, as above, with your forearms just inside your front hip bones. Now rotate your 8 laserbeams to the right corner of the room as before, and, after you lower your heels, notice how your weight is distributed evenly on both feet. Imagine you are trying to touch the ceiling with your head as you do this. Then, while maintaining contact with the ceiling and with your weight distributed equally in both feet, go onto the balls of your feet and swivel with your whole body, ie your 8 laserbeams, to the right, and then to the left. Notice how, once you have completed the first swivel, your legs are in exactly the same position underneath you as in 11.1.1, with your right foot forward and left foot back, and then, when you have completed the next swivel, your legs are in the same position, but in reverse, i.e. your left foot is now forward and your right foot back. Imagine your belly button has a laser beam coming out of it, and you are swivelling the laser beam from the wall on one side to the wall on the other (see Figures 11.3 a, b and c).

Repeat this exercise several times, returning your heels to the floor sometimes to rest your calves. Notice which, if any, body part is initiating the movement. You should realise, as you swivel on the balls of your feet, whilst maintaining your imagined contact of your head with the ceiling, that it is a

Two-beat leg press

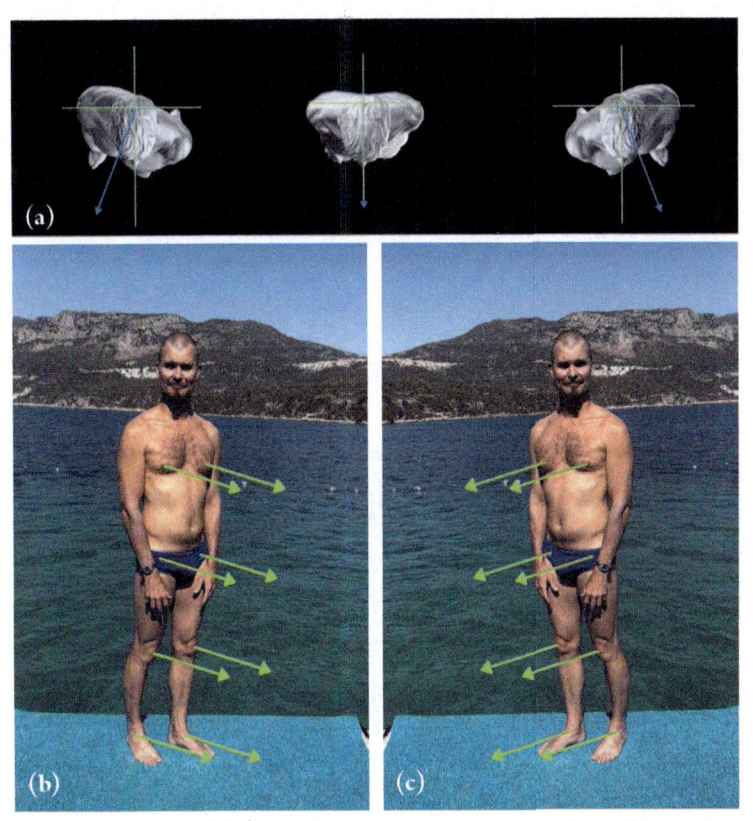

Figure 11.3: (a) Laserbeam to corner of the room from above, (b) laserbeam to left corner of the room, and (c) laserbeam to right corner of the room.

single movement: the whole body moving as one unit in order to rotate your lasers from one corner of the room to the other. It can be helpful to try to move a single body part to begin this exercise while maintaining your frame. For example, could you move your pelvis first? Could you move your shoulders first, and be able to maintain your frame? Can you move your thighs first? Generally, the answer to all these questions is no, it is impossible unless you compromise the frame.

This exercise is a rehearsal for the *Two-beat leg press* that you will learn in the water.

The SwimMastery Way

Pool activity 11.2 Counterbalance

The most efficient way of learning the correct two-beat leg press is to progress in very small steps. It is best practice to prime the nervous system with a static position first, before attempting it in movement and then in whole-stroke.

11.2.1 The swimming position

The first thing to practise is imprinting the *Counterbalance* position. This position is the swimming position: it is the position that you will hit and maintain on each and every stroke you take. You will have the same amount of rotation in each counterbalance position as you had in each *Streamline* position. Before you begin this practice in the pool, remind your body of the *Counterbalance* position that you practised on dry land. Then, push off with one arm out in front, not two. This will be the only time you will do this and makes this particular exercise easier. Determine which side you're going to start on, and make a mental note of where all of your body parts need to be to create this position, before you actually push off. If you are starting on the left, you will have the left scapula and arm forwards, the left pectoral muscle down and the left hip bone down i.e. you will be rotated to the right, and you will draw the left thigh back behind the body (see Figure 11.4) Push off directly into this position and then stand up, immediately. Gravity will cause the body to fall flat. If you notice this happening, stand up sooner, before this happens, on future repetitions. The test here is not to stay in that position for any length of time but simply to allow the nervous system to begin adapting to the skill. Then try the left side, so the right scapula sends the right arm forward, the

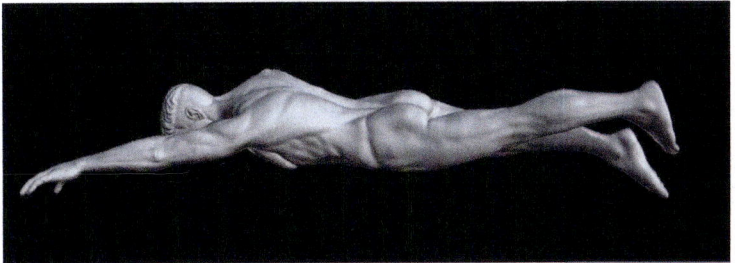

Figure 11.4: Leg behind the bodyline.

right pectoral muscle and right hip bone are down, i.e. you are rotated towards the left, and the back of the right thigh is drawn behind the body. Use the momentum from the push-off to imprint the position and then stand up, immediately.

Once you have tried this position on the left and the right, see if you can determine whether one feels easier to achieve than the other. Nine times out of ten, one side will work better, and this is the side I would start practising with. By imprinting the position on the side that feels easiest first, you can then use that as a template for the side that is less comfortable. Ultimately, you will need to work on both sides equally, it's just that you are going to begin with the side that is working better to help prime the nervous system for the task at hand. For some swimmers, this first step could take a while, and I would highly recommend patience while this skill is being imprinted.

11.2.2 Counterbalance to counterbalance

When you are able to push off from the side and immediately assume the *Counterbalance* position on one side or the other with ease, I would then suggest switching, just once. At this point, it doesn't really matter how you switch from one side to the other, i.e. your arm can come under or above the water. What is important is that you are able to go from the *Counterbalance* position on one side to the counterbalance position on the other, albeit just for a moment.

Understanding the timing here is of utmost importance. Think back to how you swivelled your lasers from one side of the room to the other in the standing rehearsal. It is one simultaneous whole-body movement, rotating you from being counterbalanced on one side to being counterbalanced on the other. Swimmers often assume that they have to use the leg to begin the rotation. However, this assumption will immediately cause a disconnect, mistime your leg movement, and create a counterbalance position that is far too wide and outside of your tube. The beginning of the rotation is created by the weight shift; once the weight shift has begun, the whole body moves as one.

Spend time allowing your nervous system to learn this skill by doing very short repeats. You can increase difficulty here by starting on different sides, ensuring you can switch with ease, regardless of which side you start on. When you are comfortable pushing off on either side, incrementally increase the number of switches that you do, whilst consistently hitting the *Counterbalance* position.

11.2.3 Add integrated breathing

Once the 'switch' step has been imprinted and you are able to hit and maintain the *Counterbalance* position in your whole stroke, you then need to add in your integrated breath. The challenge, when adding in the breath, is not to change anything in your *Counterbalance* position. This means that you will be breathing in your *Counterbalance* position, i.e. if you are breathing to the right your left scapula and arm will be forwards, your left pec and left hip bone will be down, or rotated towards the right, and your left thigh will be drawn back behind the body line. And the reverse is true for the left breath. I suggest starting with one breath first, on your preferred breathing side. Pay attention to what your legs do during that breathing stroke; are you able to keep them stable in their *Counterbalance* position? If not, you have two things to work on individually: (1) the timing and position of your integrated breath, and (2) your *Counterbalance* position. Slowly but surely, these two elements of your stroke will come together if you work on them separately.

Two beat leg press nuances

Once you are comfortable with and skilled in the above practices, you will be in a position to understand and integrate the finer aspects of this new move.

Maintain the scissor

You will have realised by now that at no point in the freestyle stroke with the *Two-Beat Leg Press* do the legs come together. During each rotation, the legs will pass each other on their way to their next *Counterbalance* position. I am often asked, "Am I not more streamlined if I have the legs together behind my torso, rather than if my legs are slightly scissored?" The key is the width of the scissor. If the legs are only as wide apart as the width of your tube i.e. your shoulders, then no, you would not be more streamlined, because your legs are still drafting within the width of the torso. But yes, if they are wider apart and outside this tube they will, of course, induce drag. This is what makes learning a correct *Two-Beat Leg Press* such a challenge, because, if it is not performed correctly, it will get in the way of your forward propulsion. The reason for never bringing the legs together, however, is because, if we did, we would then have no counterbalance to the rotation and the recovering arm, resulting in destabilisation. To test this out I suggest you try both the correct and incorrect positions in the water. Start off by pushing off in the *Counterbalance* position that is now familiar to you, notice what you feel in your body, and, most importantly, notice what happens to your rotation. Then perform the same test with your legs pressed together, i.e. not in a counterbalance position, and again notice what you feel in your body position and specifically in the degree and stability of your rotation. What you will notice is that when your legs are in the *Counterbalance* position you will be able to maintain your rotated position for a little longer, and, if you have great body awareness, you will notice that you have better access to your core muscles in this position. With the legs pressed together, the body immediately falls flat because there is no *Counterbalance*.

Apply pressure

Once the *Two-Beat Leg Press Counterbalance* position has been imprinted, with and without breathing, we are ready to think about pressure. It is important not to introduce the focus on pressure too early in this process, as this could undo all of the positional imprinting you have been working on.

When we consider pressure we simply have to think about the direction of movement and physics. Isaac Newton's Third Law of Motion states, 'for every action, there is an equal and opposite reaction'. We use this principle when applying pressure to the water with our legs. We do not want to press up and down, because the up and down motion is going to create the equal and opposite up and down direction of energy. Therefore, when teaching the fundamentals of pressure, I talk about sending the water behind the body in order to send the head forwards. It is very similar to using a fin when diving. Diving fins are very long, and if you were to attempt to just move the blade of the fin up and down you would not go very far - and you would use a lot of energy. Divers move their legs in such a way as to generate force backwards, out through the tip of the fin to send the body forwards, almost like a wave.

> **Summary of cues: Two-beat leg press**
> - Hit counterbalance: one thigh behind, one thigh in front of bodyline
> - Maintain counterbalance during arm recovery
> - Whole body switch from counterbalance to counterbalance
> - Apply pressure backwards to send head forwards

Chapter 12

Advanced Synchronisations

Up to this point, you have worked on the positioning of the body and the main movements of the parts, which set the stage for propulsion. However, it is more than the moving parts that create propulsion: it is the smooth, coordinated movement of all the parts *together* that create efficient propulsion.

You could say that this is where the magic happens. The individual parts of the stroke are essential, but they only get you so far, and so fast. The synchronisation of all of these body parts, both their positions and the movements you have worked on up until now can boost your forward momentum and, consequently, your speed. The synchronisation points we will look at in this chapter offer endless opportunities for refinement and can be worked on and improved on for years. A swimmer can make small adjustments in how different sections of the stroke are synchronised, which can have a big positive effect, but it takes time and experience to gain control over these nuances. The end result should be the synchronisation of all the elements we have discussed so far, creating a dynamic whole-body movement. This is a lifelong journey to mastery. As your body awareness and proprioception grow, so too will your ability - and desire - to better synchronise certain parts of the stroke.

I will cover each synchronisation point in isolation. To begin with, it is almost impossible to coordinate all the points together. Therefore, breaking them down and working on two aspects at a time (pairs) is the best way to create an effective propulsion system. It is the coordination of all the movements that will lead to the 'magic'. As you understand and develop these nuances and the neurological pathways become stronger, the water will begin to feel thicker, while the movement through the water and the stroke will feel more fluid and effortless. As you cycle through the pairs, you will start to notice how they match up with each other, allowing your stroke to develop into a finely tuned and integrated whole-body movement, resulting in more forward propulsion for the same, or even less, energy cost.

Five Propulsive Parts

1. Rotation (R)
2. Entry (E)
3. Extension (X)
4. Catch (C)
5. Leg Press (L)

The Synchronisation Combinations

- Rotation and Entry (RE)
- Rotation and Extension (RX)
- Rotation and Catch (RC)
- Entry and Catch (EC)
- Rotation and Legs (RL)
- Legs and Catch (LC)
- Legs and Extension (LE)

I strongly advise that you work on these pairs in order, to begin with. When embarking on the synchronisation journey, concentrating on - or starting with - the perceived propulsive parts of the stroke, such as Catch and Leg press, can be very tempting. However, this is very likely to lead to a mistimed stroke because of the natural human instinct to 'pull' and 'kick'. If you ensure that rotation is the key focus as you begin to move through the pairs, then you will minimise any risk of reverting to old habits.

Review of Earlier Skills

Before moving on to the pairings, review all the skills you have been practising. This will ensure that you are able to begin synchronising the right movements.

Rotation and Weight Shift

In our view, the rotation is the power source, or the engine, of the whole stroke. The rotation begins with the weight shift, and that shift is caused by the scapula and recovery arm moving forwards of the rib cage, as well as the angle of rotation that the body is in during this phase. You should tune into this moment where the weight shift happens, and take advantage of the energy created by rotating your whole body and sending the energy forwards through your middle *Trident*. Every synchronisation pairing that you ever think about will build on sending your energy forwards in this way.

Entry Position

The entry connects to the rotation and weight shift. Executed correctly, initiated by the weight shift, the whole body rotates, and the entering arm straightens as the scapula sends the fingernails to the front wall of the pool. These two synchronisation points happen at exactly the same time as the entry receives the force generated by the rotation and channels or directs it forwards. A wonderful cue to use during this practice is; to rotate and straighten the arm, which can be shortened to rotate and straighten or rotate fingernails to the wall.

Extension

Extension is the *Streamline* position, which is at the end of whole body rotation, with the leading arm straight and the fingernails forward. It is at the moment that the body hits *Streamline* that you direct all of the force that has been created during the rotation and the extending of the arm into forward momentum. Channel the force out through the head, the *Streamline* side scapula and fingernails, and the scapula of the recovery arm. These represent the three points of the *Trident*. A common error when focusing on extension is to overextend or overreach. This will cause the arm to become disconnected because the ribcage will tilt posteriorly, causing the scapula to move backwards and the pelvis to move into an anterior tilt. This results in the swimmer being disconnected along the body and sending all of the force they had created off to one side and upwards.

Catch

The catch creates the resistance against which the body levers forward at the moment of weight shift and whole-body rotation. The key point to remember here is to maintain the position of the upper part of the *Streamline* arm as you fold at the elbow, so that energy can be channelled forward when rotation begins. This will enable you to anchor onto the largest amount of water, and apply the maximum amount of pressure safely.

Leg Press

The legs serve two main purposes.

Firstly, they are the anchor point around which the whole body rotates. Linked to this anchoring function, the legs also help control the amount of whole-body rotation. They allow the body to stop swivelling at a certain point, allowing you to control the *Streamline* position and direct the energy forwards.

Secondly, the legs can also provide a small amount of propulsion. While pressing backwards, you will be sending the energy forwards out through the head, or middle *Trident* (Newton's Law).

After reviewing these individual parts of the stroke, it is time to combine them and practise synchronising the movements.

Synchronisation Combinations

Rotation and Entry (RE)

It is at the entry point, the *Cuckoo* position, that the first synchronisation takes place. The whole high side of the body – made up of the entering arm, the same side scapula, the same side hip and the same side leg – will rotate and send the entering arm to extension.

A great cue to use for this synchronisation point is to rotate the whole body, the scapula sending the fingernails forwards, and allowing the rotation to straighten the arm. An advanced thought process for these movements is to ensure that the end of the rotation finishes at exactly the same time as the fingernails reach their extended position. As I have mentioned, it is very easy to overdo the extension. Try to feel what the scapula does at the end of the extension - there should be no tension in the shoulder area at extension (see Figure 12.2).

Once you have practised these cues several times and feel the synchronisation, perform the same movement, and channel

Figure 12.1: Rotation and Entry (RE).

the energy forwards through the middle prong of the *Trident*, i.e. the head. This helps eliminate the common error of trying to reach through the extending arm, which results in disconnecting the arm from the torso, which sends your energy in the wrong direction. Now move on to thinking about channelling your energy simultaneously through the middle Trident and the streamline *Trident*, i.e. the top of the head and the *Streamline* side.

> ### Cues for RE
>
> » Rotate and allow this movement to straighten the arm
> » Rotate the middle *Trident* forwards
> » Rotate the middle *Trident* and streamline *Trident* forwards

Rotation and Extension (RX)

With this synchronisation point, you will focus on the end of the movement you have just practised in RE. Synchronise the end of the rotation with the extension. You are aiming to hit your optimal rotated streamlined position at the same point that your fingernails touch the wall (see Figure 12.2).

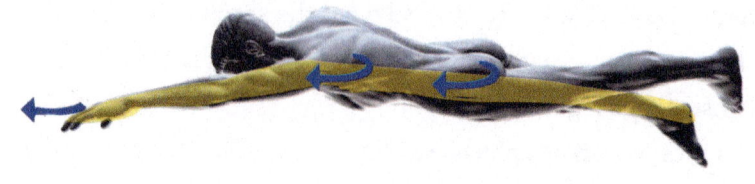

Figure 12.2: Rotation and Extension (RX).

> ### Cues for RX
>
> » Rotate the fingernails to the front end of the pool
> » Rotate the middle *Trident* and streamline *Trident* forwards

Rotation and Catch (RC)

In RC you are focusing on synchronising the beginning of the hold, i.e. once the *Streamline* arm has folded and begun pressing on the water, with the beginning of the rotation. As we have already talked about in the *Catch* section, the catch should already be formed and ready to apply pressure at the moment when the rotation or weight shift begins. Apply pressure to the rung of the ladder or upon the ball at the same moment you begin the rotation. Then add in the middle *Trident* thought process to ensure the energy you have created through this synchronisation point is being channelled forwards through the head (see Figure 12.3).

Figure 12.3: Rotation and Catch (RC).

> ### Cues for RC
>
> » Rotate and press the *Catch* arm at the same time
> » Send the energy forwards through the middle *Trident*

Entry and Catch (EC)

In EC you are aiming to apply pressure on the *Catch* arm at exactly the same time that the entering arm begins to straighten (initiated by the weight shift). These two parts of the body are separated by the torso – the rotation is the implied third element of this combination. Consciously focus on the two arms while unconsciously supporting both through the rotation. In order to maintain the connection of each arm through the scapula to the torso, it is advisable to spend some time focusing on both scapulae staying forwards through the very first part of this movement (see Figure 12.4).

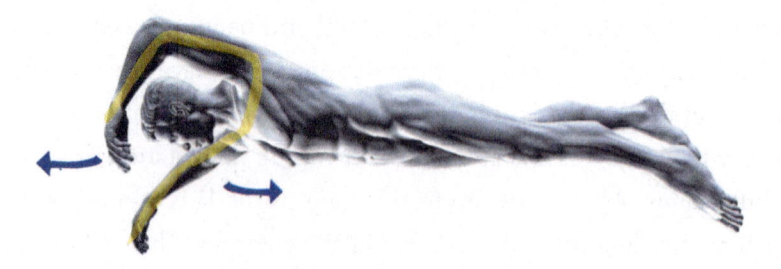

Figure 12.4: Entry and Catch (EC).

A common error, as discussed in the *Catch* section, is for the swimmer to 'pull' the catching arm through the water before the rotation, which results in the disconnecting of the arm. Focus on keeping the scapula forward during the first part of this synchronisation point to prevent this.

Cues for EC

- » Keep both scapulae forward the moment the rotation begins
- » As you apply pressure to the *Catch*, allow the rotation to straighten the entering arm

Rotation and Legs (RL)

In RL you will examine the synchronisation of the body's rotation from *Streamline* on one side to *Streamline* on the other, and the changing *Counterbalance* positions of the legs. As the whole body

Advanced Synchronisations

rotation begins, consciously apply pressure with the leg on the starting *Streamline* side whilst simultaneously drawing the other leg behind the body into its *Counterbalance* position. Starting in a right-side *Streamline*, you will apply pressure with the right leg, and send the left leg behind the body, ending up in a left *Streamline* with your legs in their *Counterbalance* position. Starting in a left-side *Streamline*, you will apply pressure with the left leg, and send the right leg behind the body, ending up in a right *Streamline* with your legs in their *Counterbalance* position. Channel the force generated by this combination forward through the head, i.e. the middle *Trident*. Aim to end in your best *Streamline Counterbalance* position (see Figure 12.5a and b).

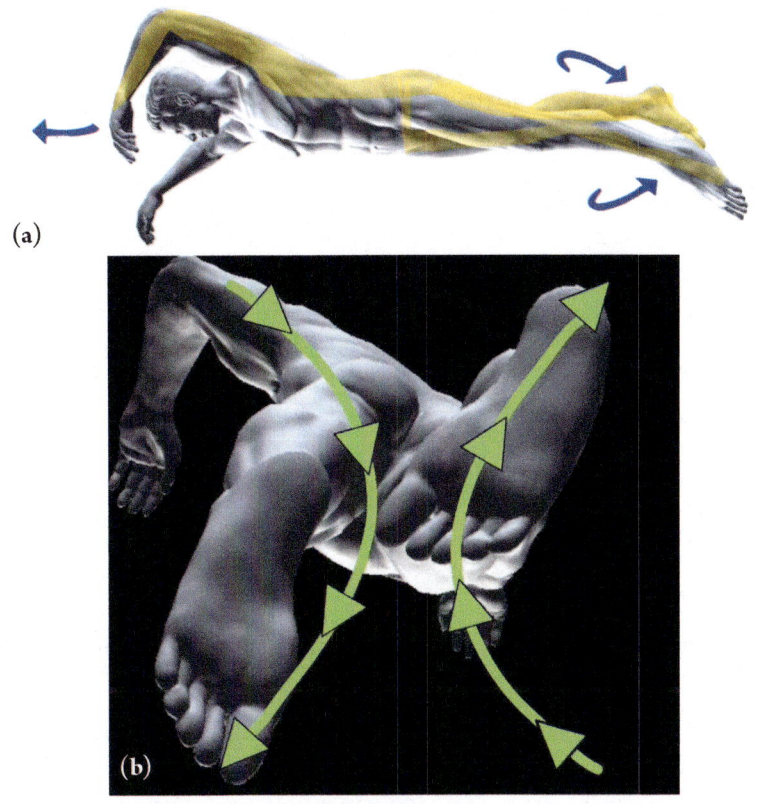

Figure 12.5: (a) Rotation and Legs (RL) and (b) Rotation and Legs (RL) from behind.

> **Cues for RL**
>
> » Rotate and apply pressure with the *Streamline* side leg
> » Send the energy generated forwards through the middle *Trident*
> » Finish with the legs in the *Counterbalance* position

Legs and Catch (LC)

In LC the legs and the *Catch* are separated by the torso – the rotation is the implied third member of this combination. Consciously focus on applying pressure on the catching arm and the pressing leg at the same time, using the pressure on both of these as anchors to rotate the body and move forwards past the 'held' water. Make sure the other leg goes to its *Counterbalance* position. Channel the energy generated by this combination forwards out through the head i.e. the middle *Trident*. Aim to end in your best *Streamline Counterbalance* position (see Figure 12.6).

Figure 12.6: Legs and Catch (LC).

> **Cues for LC**
>
> » Feel the pressure on the catching arm and the pressing leg at the same time
> » Send the energy forwards out through the middle *Trident* prong
> » Finish in a *Streamline Counterbalance* position

Advanced Synchronisations

Legs and Extension (LE)

In LE the legs and entry are separated by the torso – the rotation is the implied third member of this combination. Consciously focus on applying pressure on the leg and aiming to finish the press of the leg at the same moment you reach extension. Channel the energy generated by this combination out through the head, i.e. the middle *Trident* prong. Aim to end in your best *Streamline Counterbalance* position. (see Figure 12.7).

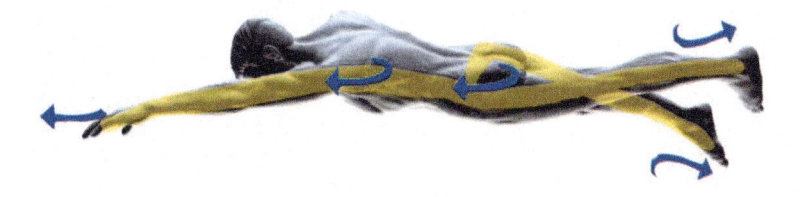

Figure 12.7: Legs and Extension (LE).

Cues for LE

» Aim to finish the press of leg and hitting extension at the exact same moment
» Channel the energy forwards through the middle *Trident* and *Streamline Trident*
» Finish in a *Streamline Counterbalance* position

Let's first practise the standing rehearsal that you can use for each of the synchronisation points. You will then focus on one combination at a time.

The SwimMastery Way

Dryland activity 12.1

12.1.1 Standing Rehearsal for Synchronisation

Standing in your *Streamline Counterbalance* position, head to the ceiling and scapula sending fingernails to the ceiling, put the other arm into the entry point, the *Cuckoo* position. Then allow the *Streamline* arm to fold at the elbow and form the start of the *Catch* position (see Figure 12.8).

Then, go up onto the balls of your feet and simply swivel the whole body, sending the arrow out of your belly button from one corner of the room to the other. Simultaneously straighten the *Cuckoo* arm, sending the fingernails to the ceiling and allowing the *Catch* arm to follow its *Catch* pathway and end up with the forearm just inside your hip bone. Through the swivelling motion, the legs will automatically perform the correct pathway for the *Two-Beat Leg Press*.

Figure 12.8: Wholestroke Standing rehearsal - beginning of synchronisation point.

Pool activity 12.1

12.1.1 Single Arm Drill

The single arm drill, performed correctly, is an ideal opportunity to master the synchronisation combinations.

The drill is very complex, so any mistimed movements are very obvious because you should instantly feel a loss of the connection through the whole body that you have worked on and experienced until now. These insights will help you to discover which combinations you need to work on.

Keep the left forearm just inside your hip bone (as you did in *Build the Frame Without Arms* drill) so that it is out of the way and cannot participate in the movement of the body. You will need to use a relaxed *Flutter* throughout this drill.

Now, starting in left side Streamline, ensure that your scapula has sent your fingernails to the front wall of the pool. *Form your Catch* position by folding at the elbow and pause for a moment. Then simultaneously rotate the whole body and apply pressure to the catching arm, sending the energy forwards and out through the middle *Trident*, your head. You should now be rotated on the other side, with both forearms inside your hip bones as in *Build the Frame Without Arms*. Pause in this position. Then recover the left arm, and, once it reaches its *Cuckoo* position, rotate the whole body to straighten the arm, sending the energy forwards through the middle and left *Trident* prongs. Pause again (see Figure 12.9).

When executing the *Single Arm* drill it is very important that it is the rotation of the whole body (shoulders to feet) that is setting the stroke in motion, not the arm pulling the body round.

Once you have learned how to do the *Single Arm* drill, you use it to focus on each of the synchronisation combinations apart from EC.

Now, for each synchronisation combination, gradually remove the pauses, first removing the pause with both arms

The SwimMastery Way

inside the hip bones, then removing the pause at the *Catch*, leaving you with one pause in *Streamline*. I recommend you maintain the pause at Streamline until you feel you are beginning to master the synchronisation combinations. Only then would I suggest removing the pause at *Streamline*. You might find that you can remove the pauses sooner with some combinations than others.

Focus on just one synchronisation combination at a time, e.g. rotation and *Catch* (RC). For each combination, there are two pairings. With this combination, there is 'rotation and left *Catch*' and there is 'rotation and right *Catch*'. Initially, focus on just one of these pairings, i.e. either left or right, for several repeats or minutes, and then switch to focus on the other pairing.

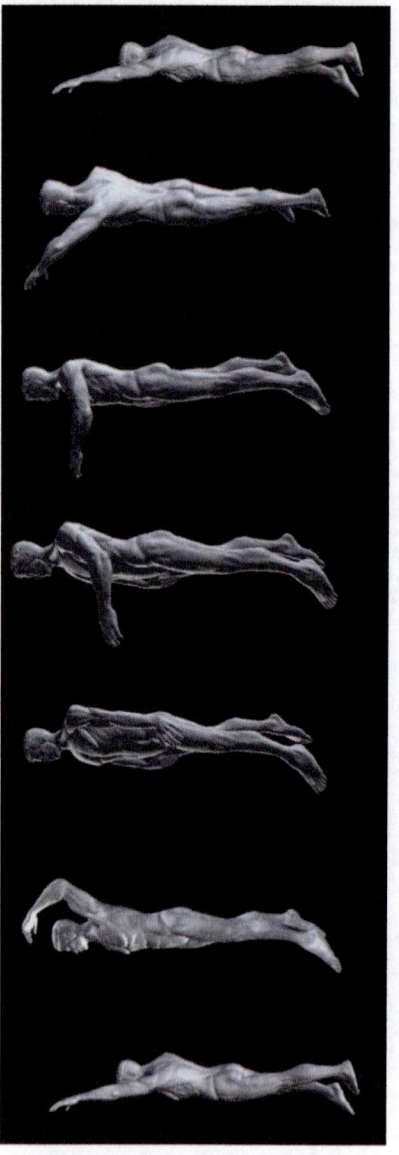

Figure 12.9: Single Arm Drill sequence.

Pool activity 12.2

12.2.1 Whole Stroke with Gradually Expanding Focus

In this activity, you will use whole stroke but your attention will be focused on just one combination. At first, you will follow the Single Arm drill with whole stroke practice of the same combination.

Rather than jumping right into whole-stroke swimming where you may be tempted to try to monitor and refine many combinations at once, we can start with a very small area of focus and gradually increase the field of view and control. Here is a way to incrementally increase the challenge:

» Focus on just one synchronisation combination, e.g. rotation and catch (RC). For every stroke cycle, there are two pairings for each combination. For example, with this combination there is 'rotation and left Catch' and there is 'rotation and right Catch'. Initially, focus on just one of those pairings (either left or right) for several repeats or minutes, and then switch to focus on the other pairing.

» Progress through the combinations in this sequence:
- Focus on combinations that are adjacent to one another, e.g. leg and rotation (LR)
- Focus on combinations that are across the body / contralateral, e.g. Catch and entry (CE)
- Focus on combinations that are on the same side of the body, e.g. leg and Catch (LC)

» Blend two synchronisation combinations together, e.g. leg and rotation (LR), rotation and entry (RE).

Working through these synchronisation combinations is a lifelong journey, with endless opportunities to improve stroke timing whilst maintaining whole body connection. Mastery of them will result in a more fluid, a faster and a more energy-efficient swimming technique (see Figure 12.10).

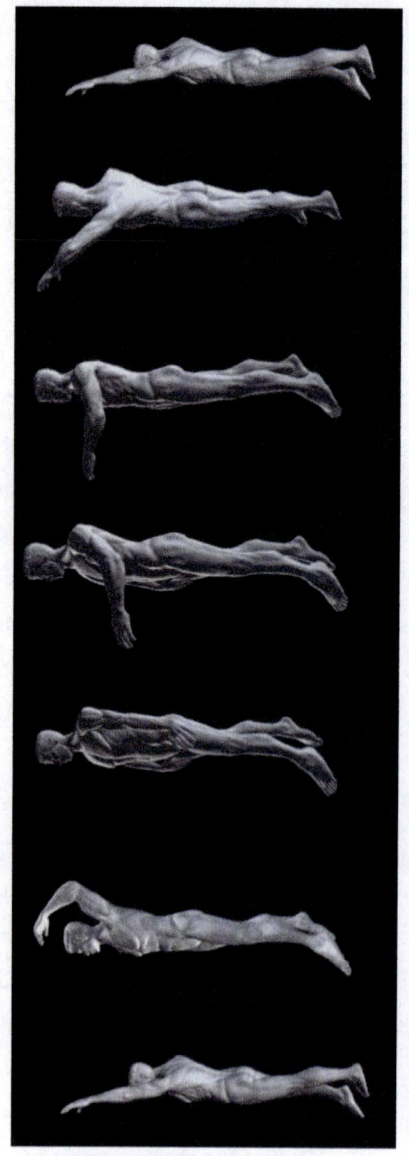

Figure 12.10: Whole Stroke synchronisation sequence.

Chapter 13

Speed

Who doesn't want to go faster? I think that, even if we have other primary goals that are more important to us, secretly we would all be ecstatic if the stopwatch showed quicker times. But the harder you chase speed, the less you actually achieve it. It is a conundrum that swimmers and swim coaches have been trying to solve for decades. More often than not the strategy has been to increase power and energy input by applying maximum strength and increasing stroke rate (tempo) in the hope of achieving faster times. However, the faster we go, the more resistance we create, so these attempts are often futile, resulting in very tired and disappointed swimmers - and coaches.

Let's think about how swimming, which we do in the medium of water, actually works. The space in front of the swimmer is taken up by water and, in order for the swimmer to pass through it, the water has to move out of the swimmer's way to make space for the swimmer's body. At low speeds and tempos this causes less of a problem as the water has more time to move out of the way, but as the speed and tempo (stroke rate) increases, so too does the resistance caused as a result of the water not having time to move out of the swimmer's way. If you add a messy, discombobulated and disconnected stroke to the equation, this increased resistance becomes the determining factor in the speed conundrum.

If we take running or cycling as an example, building strength, increasing energy input and upping the tempo or cadence, *will* result in faster speeds. The difference between these sports and swimming is that water is 800 times denser than air, and therefore not as easy to move through. So the only effective way to gain greater speed in water is to ensure that you create the sleekest vessel possible to cut through the water, thus allowing the water to move out of the way more easily, causing less resistance. Then you need to maintain this shape as you increase tempo and, through that, speed.

A research study for the US Navy Seals measured the efficiency of the swimming technique of a dolphin. Using the best available assessment tools, they determined that a dolphin was 80% efficient in water, i.e. from 100% of energy input they were able to transfer 80% into forward movement. In contrast, humans are only able to transfer a maximum of 9% or 10% of our energy input into forward movement in swimming. And 9% or 10% efficiency is achieved by less than 2% of the swimming population, the likes of Michael Phelps, for example. The rest of us can transfer a mere 2% or 3% of the 100% energy input into forward movement. Let's think about that for a moment. It means that 97% of the energy a swimmer puts into their stroke is not transferred into forward movement. Given that most of us will only achieve 3% efficiency, we must make the most of it. And the harder we try, and the more disconnected we become when we swim, the less likely we are to achieve our potential 3%.

Therefore, to gain speed, we must stay true to the shape we present to the water, at all costs. How do we do that? We turn to maths.

Working with metrics

Finding your optimisation equation is the key to real speed in the pool. This optimisation equation is made up of several metrics for each distance you want to swim: strokes per length, tempo, and the optimal perceived effort. Increasing your stroke rate alone will, firstly, give you no measure of whether you have been able to maintain form and, secondly, will only serve to tire you out. So it is not generally effective. Because we only have a maximum opportunity of about 3% efficiency to play with, we must maintain form and our optimal stroke length as we increase tempo. For us to sustain and measure this, the perceived effort has to be taken into account.

The quickest route to gaining speed in the pool is working on each element in isolation first.

By now, you will have progressed with your technique, including body position and well-timed synchronisations. Now, we will introduce each of the elements of speed separately before bringing them together. Ultimately, though, the ability to work on these metrics together creates the magic that results in increased speed.

What are the key metrics?

- Stroke count - Strokes per length (SPL)
- Tempo - seconds per stroke (Mode 1 on the Finis Tempo Trainer)
- Rest
- RPE - Rate of Perceived Exertion
- Distance
- Time

Using your data for improvement: recording, analysing, and decision making

We recommend using a waterproof notebook or having your set printed onto waterproof paper or inside a plastic sleeve, and keeping this at one end of the pool during each swim session. This way, you can easily note down your data each time you get back to that end of the pool, and it is a powerful, in-the-moment accountability tool.

The data that you record during your sessions will enable you, with the support of your coach, to make the best decisions on changes that will lead you most effectively towards your swimming goals. The best virtual swim coach will be able to support you by analysing this data, designing appropriate swim sets, and advising on the cues you currently need, wherever you and they are in the world.

Stroke count

We begin by becoming familiar with stroke count. This is a skill in itself, which needs targeted practice to allow the brain to adapt to eventually being able to count strokes in the background automatically. The easiest way to count your strokes is to push off the wall and begin counting from the first arm entry. Ensuring that your push-off distance is the same each time is crucial for consistency and more exact measurements and records.

Start by practising stroke counting for single lengths at a time. Making this your sole focus is advisable rather than having a stroke technique cue alongside it. Once you can easily count your strokes consistently for one length at a time, then increase the distance to two lengths, and practise counting strokes per length over this distance until this, too, becomes automated. Then, incrementally increase the distance as your brain adapts to this new skill. When you can count your strokes consistently for 200m with ease, either by counting individual 25s or by counting continuously for the 200m, go back to single lengths and, this time, add a technique cue with the counting. Once again, incrementally increase the distance, always remembering that any goal we set should be achievable, even if it is mentally taxing at first.

Swim Watches

You may have a watch or other device to give you metrics during your swims. Most of these devices do have the option to count strokes for you. There are a couple of reasons why we do not recommend relying on the watch for stroke counting, preferring that you count them yourself.

1. The watches can only count the movement of one arm and, therefore, count 2 arm entries (one right arm and one left arm) as a single stroke. Because we sometimes start and finish stroking on different arms, your stroke count may be out by up to 3 strokes if we start and finish on the non-wearing arm, which is significant if you are only swimming 25m/yd repeats. Counting each arm entry is the most accurate way to count.

2. You can only see the data on the watch at the end of the length or, worse still, once you get home and can download the data onto another device. This means that you are not aware of your stroke count in the moment, so you cannot take the opportunity to make immediate changes to your technique that may positively affect your stroke and potentially reduce your stroke count there and then!

However, the watches can be really useful for collecting data on other metrics, such as speed and distance. You will find recording this sort of data useful when you analyse changes over a period of time.

Stroke tempo

The next metric to work on is your stroke tempo. Your best friend in the pool, outside of your own body, is the Finis Tempo Trainer. It is a small device which rhythmically beeps, very similar to a metronome

The SwimMastery Way

that a pianist would use, placed inside your swim cap. You can set the frequency of the beep to any interval you like, depending on how much time you would like each stroke to take. We recommend using the Tempo Trainer on Mode 1, which sets the timer to seconds per stroke. Two other modes are available on this device, which we don't recommend using.

We need to train the brain to stroke on the beep. To do this, we make the beep from the Tempo Trainer our *only* focus for single lengths at a time until those new neurological pathways are established enough to automatically maintain the rhythm and timing of the stroke. Consider using a starting tempo of between 1.20 and 1.40 seconds per stroke, depending on the tempo you are currently accustomed to. For many of you, this may feel relatively slow to begin with, but it is wise to learn to match your stroke to the tempo at a slower pace, which enables faster learning. Set your Tempo Trainer and push off the wall, counting the beeps. Your first stroke will begin on the third beep. Then, swim the rest of the length, synchronising your whole body rotation to the beep. The information booklet accompanying the Tempo Trainer suggests timing your hand entry to the beep; however, it is much easier to maintain the technique you have worked on up until this point if you begin by synchronising the rotation to the beep. Of course, you have already discovered in the Advanced Synchronisations chapter that all parts of the stroke are, in fact, timed with each other. Therefore, ultimately you will be able to match any synchronisation point to the beep.

Stroke count and tempo

You can blend the two metrics once you feel comfortable swimming to the tempo trainer for multiple lengths. Set the tempo trainer to anything between 1.20 and 1.40 seconds per stroke (whatever feels most comfortable) and swim the length, rotating to the beep, and this time count your strokes as well. Repeat these single lengths until you can consistently swim to the beep while counting strokes. Then, incrementally increase the distance as your skill increases. Once you feel comfortable with both these metrics, add a cue, ensuring you can still rotate to the beep and count strokes.

Rest

I like swimmers to think of the rest as a 'trading chip' when swimming long distances. Can you imagine how hard it would be to maintain focus if you were to swim 1500m in the pool with no rest intervals? And it would be harder still if you were doing this in the 25 metre or yard pool. My guess is that, very quickly, your mind would start to wander to other things, such as what you have to do at work that day or jobs you may have to do around the house. Swimming up and down a short course pool for that long is not very exciting, so boredom and tedium will inevitably kick in. We need to remember that when we are not focused on our swimming and improving our technique or working on specific metrics, our body will always revert to our default technique, and swimming with no focus only offers the opportunity to imprint the default technique more deeply.

We already know that the only successful way to swim faster is by improving technique, and the only way to improve technique is to keep our minds focused on the task at hand. The key to achieving this is to break your swim down into bite-sized chunks that will allow you to stay focused. It may mean, to begin with, you are swimming many 25s or sets of 50s, putting the required amount of rest between these repeats to stay focused on the next repeat. As your brain and body adapt to the task, so will your ability to stay focused for longer. You can then start to reduce the amount of rest between each repeat until the rest is so short that you can increase the distance of the repeat, for example from 25m repeats to 100m repeats, and so on, as below:

- 4 x 25 with 20 seconds rest after each 25
- 4 x 25 with 10 seconds rest after each 25
- 2 x 50 with 20 seconds rest after each 50
- 2 x 50 with 10 seconds rest after each 50
- 3 x 100 with 30 seconds rest after each 100
- 3 x 100 with 20 seconds rest after each 100
- 3 x 100 with 10 seconds rest after each 100

A measure of when to decrease rest time is when you can nose breathe (inhale and exhale) with ease (see Chapter 3: Air Exchange) during the rest period and feel ready for the next repeat.

Rate of Perceived Exertion (RPE)

This metric is purely subjective, using a scale of 1 to 5. Over time you will become familiar with how your body feels while swimming, and we recommend relating this to how it feels when you exercise on land. For example:

- RPE of 1 could be equated to a brisk walk.
- RPE of 2 to jogging
- RPE of 3 to running where you could still hold a conversation
- RPE of 4 to running at a faster pace
- RPE of 5 would be full-out sprinting (anaerobic).

Rate of Perceived Effort (RPE)

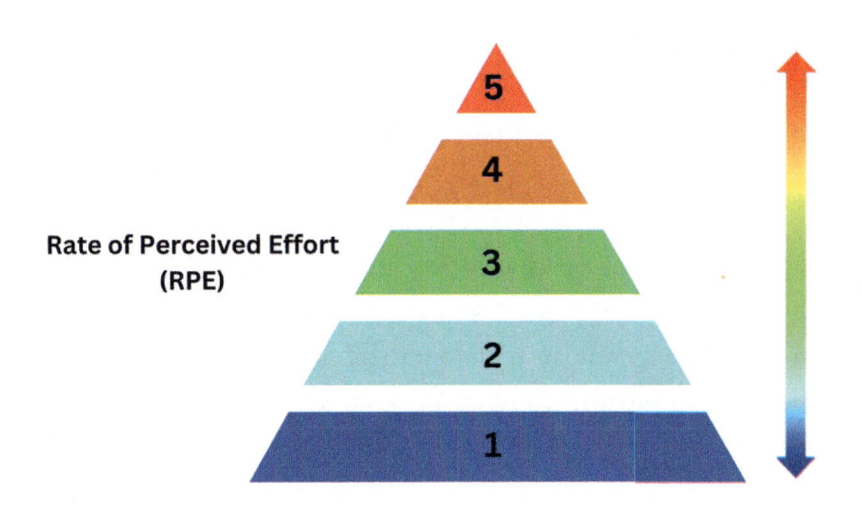

It is advisable to spend most of your swim practice time in the lower RPE levels, with at most 10% of the time and distance in RPE 4 and never to reach RPE level 5 during practice. At the lower end of the RPE scale, you will be better placed to maintain focus and therefore to continue to improve your technique. At the top of the RPE scale, you will be working at a higher intensity level and may more easily revert to using your default stroke. So, spending more time at the higher RPE levels will result in increased aerobic fitness, but the technique will not change or improve. In fact, RPE level 5 should only be reached by swimmers who are sprinting, i.e. 50 m and 100 m.

Find your own RPE scale by swimming at different intensities and giving each level a number out of 5. Do this by increasing the tempo using the tempo trainer and/or controlling the pressure during the *Catch* and *Two-beat leg press* (see Chapters 10 and 11). You will need to repeat this exercise several times to begin to see a pattern in what your own RPE scale is. If you use a watch that measures Heart Rate in the water, after your sessions where you swim at different intensities in this way, you might find it helpful to calibrate your subjective sense of RPE against the 'Time in Heart Rate Zones' shown in the data from your watch.

Distance

The distance you choose to swim should always be based on two things.

Firstly, you must take your end goal into account when you are planning on what distance you are going to swim in the pool for practice. For example, if you are planning on swimming a 3.8 km swim in an Ironman triathlon, then, of course, it is important to ensure that the distances you are swimming in practice are going to enable you to achieve this end goal. Having said that, I don't recommend swimming long repeats without rest in a swimming pool. It is not necessary, leads to a loss of focus and deterioration of the stroke, and allows too much opportunity to imprint bad habits. Therefore, I recommend repeating short distances and reducing the rest, as described above.

Secondly, what is the task at hand? What is the process you want to improve? Are you beginning to work on a new element of your stroke? If this is the case, the distances you swim should be short so you can maintain focus on this new element. Suppose you are working on stroke count per length or tempo: in that case, it is advisable to begin with short distances and then, when you are easily achieving the desired stroke count and tempo while still maintaining form, incrementally increase the distance. The idea is always to set an achievable goal that pushes you just outside of your comfort zone but not so far out of your comfort zone that the task becomes unachievable and your stroke deteriorates, which results in negative imprinting. An unachievable task has two likely consequences: demotivation and/or demoralisation, and a greater possibility of imprinting a disorganised stroke.

As a marathon runner would never run a series of marathon distances in training for that event; as a swimmer, you do not need to swim the distance of any event you have entered to be able to swim the distance on the day. Indeed, this can be counterproductive due to the risk of losing form, imprinting bad habits and increasing the risk of injury. So I recommend increasing the distance of your swims relative to the distance of the planned event. Over the increased distance, circle through your A, B, and C cues every 50 strokes or between buoys. If, for instance, you were entering your first Ironman (3.8km), I recommend building up to swim a continuous 3km in a lake or ocean (depending on where your event is being held) a month before the event. If you are new to open water, it is also essential that you familiarise yourself with all aspects of open water swimming: cold, sighting, depth, distance, wetsuit, feeding etc.

Time

Time is a metric that many swimmers become obsessed with. However, focusing on this metric can be the very reason that you never actually achieve better times. I will explain using an example of one of my swimmers. I was leading a swim practice, and I happened to be standing in front of the third lane, where one of my swimmers was doing the set we had put up on the board. The set required the swimmer to swim three 50s. On the first 50, we asked the swimmers to swim easy and record their time and count their strokes. We asked the swimmers to descend the next two 50s, swimming the second 50 at a moderate pace and the third 50 fast, once again asking them to time each 50 and count the strokes for each 50.

It was one of the most interesting swim sets I have ever had the pleasure of observing. Watching the human instinctive need to work hard to go faster was fascinating. The swimmer set off on the first 50 with a beautiful, integrated and well-timed stroke. The water remained smooth and still, and the swim stroke was silent. He finished this first 50, looked up at the pace clock and smiled: 45 seconds with 34 strokes. After 20 seconds of rest, he set off for the second 50, trying to swim at a moderate pace. He pushed off and began swimming the length with relative ease; his stroke still looked somewhat organised, and although definitely noisier, it was still pretty quiet, and there was not too much splash. He touched the wall and looked up at the pace clock again. It was 40 seconds. He smiled again, thrilled. He had taken 38 strokes for this 50. I could almost see his brain at work during these next 20 seconds of rest. It seemed he was thinking he had this in the bag, as he had taken five seconds off for the second 50, and he was ecstatic. He looked at the pace clock, pushed off ready to begin his third 50. What happened next was nothing short of hilarious! The entire lane turned into what I can only describe as a Jacuzzi®! Arms and legs were thrashing, sending splash everywhere, and the noise was noticeably more than in the previous two 50s. He thrashed his way back down the length, touched the wall and looked up at the pace clock. I will never forget his face. It started with a look of pure elation and anticipation, and then, as he noticed the time on the pace clock, it turned to utter disappointment and despair.

45 seconds! And his stroke count had gone up to 42! He was crushed. It was what had happened in his brain that had caused this outcome. When he decided he had to go all out and swim that last 50 fast, his beautiful technique went out of the window, and he became a pulling, kicking, thrashing human instinct-driven swimmer who was trying to work as hard as he possibly could, to go as fast as he possibly could. This resulted in him swimming at the same speed as when he set off for that first easy 50! But he had used a great deal more energy! Nothing illustrated more clearly the futility of trying too hard. It's a story I relate to all my clients in the hope that it will help them to realise that when we think about going fast and use the pace clock as our primary metric, it often results in a loss of connection through the body and therefore simply churning up the water, creating more resistance and using a lot more energy, with no increase in speed whatsoever.

In the early stages, leave the metric of speed as a by-product of the other metrics. As your stroke becomes more efficient, it will lengthen, reducing your stroke count. As this becomes more deeply imprinted, so will your ability to swim with your new or improved technique at faster and faster tempos. This will always result in faster swim times. If you stay true to the principle of not compromising your technique on your journey to swimming faster, you will swim faster. That is guaranteed. It is just a mathematical equation. If you maintain your stroke length at a faster tempo, you will swim quicker times.

Everyone is swimming for different reasons and has different goals that are potentially constantly evolving and changing as the swimming skill level moves up the spiral. We hope that you are able to continue to use the information in this book to keep improving your body awareness, technique both in terms of understanding the correct positions to keep your joints safe as well as in your actual stroke and then use the principles that we have touched on in this chapter to swim more fluidly, efficiently and with more ease than you ever thought possible. The by-product of all of the above can only be: you will get faster!

Appendix 1

Sample Swim Session Plans

Standard Pool

Theme: Build the Frame
- **Level 1**
- **Main sets total distance: 1200y/m**

Main Set 1: Build the Frame No Arms (600y/m)

Cues	A	Head to foot alignment (feel tall, tilt pelvis if necessary)
	B	Release the head (turn off the muscles in the back of the neck so the head floats in a neutral position)
	C	Inside of elbows resting on rib cage

Drills: 1 length with each cue, probably 4 repeats in each length, stand up after each drill repeat.

A	
B	
C	
Choice	

Short whole stroke repeats: 6 whole strokes, no breathing, stand up, repeat to end of length.

4 × 4 × 25	Rep 1	Rep 2	Rep 3	Rep 4
A				
B				
C				
Choice				

Whole stroke repeats with breathing

When adding breathing, keep your focus on the cue and try not to change your focus to breathing.

2 × 4 × 25	A	B	C	Choice
First 6 strokes no breathing, rest of length add breathing				
Breathing for the entire length				

Main Set 2: Build the Frame With Arms (600y/m)

Cues	A	Arms are extensions of your scapula
	B	Slide the scapula in the direction of travel
	C	Allow the scapula to take the fingernails forward as if touching something in front of you

Drills: 1 length with each cue, probably 4 repeats in each length, stand up after each drill repeat.

A	
B	
C	
Choice	

Short whole stroke repeats: 6 whole strokes, no breathing, stand up, repeat to end of length.

4 × 4 × 25	Rep 1	Rep 2	Rep 3	Rep 4
A				
B				
C				
Choice				

Whole stroke repeats with breathing

When adding breathing, keep your focus on the cue and try not to change your focus to breathing.

2 × 4 × 25	A	B	C	Choice
First 6 strokes no breathing, rest of length add breathing				
Breathing for the entire length				

Theme: Build the Frame
- **Level 2**
- **Main sets total distance: 1600y/m**

Main Set 1: Build the Frame No Arms (800y/m)

Cues	A	Head to foot alignment (feel tall, tilt pelvis if necessary)
	B	Release the head (turn off the muscles in the back of the neck so the head floats in a neutral position)
	C	Inside of elbows resting on rib cage

Whole stroke repeats with breathing

When breathing, keep your focus on the cue and try not to change your focus to breathing.

*First 6 strokes no breathing

	A	B	C	Choice
*4 × 25				
4 × 25				
4 × 50				
4 × 25				

	A + B	A + C	B + C	A + B + C
4 × 25				
4 × 50				

Main Set 2: Build the Frame With Arms (800y/m)

Cues	A	Arms are extensions of your scapula
	B	Slide the scapula in the direction of travel
	C	Allow the scapula to take the fingernails forward as if touching something in front of you

Whole stroke repeats with breathing

When breathing, keep your focus on the cue and try not to change your focus to breathing.

*First 6 strokes no breathing

	A	B	C	Choice
*4 × 25				
4 × 25				
4 × 50				
4 × 25				

	A + B	A + C	B + C	A + B + C
4 × 25				
4 × 50				

Theme: Build the Frame

- **Level 3**
- **Main sets total distance: 1800y/m**

Main Set 1: Build the Frame No Arms (900y/m)

Cues	A	Head to foot alignment (feel tall, tilt pelvis if necessary)
	B	Release the head (turn off the muscles in the back of the neck so the head floats in a neutral position)
	C	Inside of elbows resting on rib cage

Whole stroke repeats with breathing

When breathing, keep your focus on the cue and try not to change your focus to breathing.

*First 6 strokes no breathing

	A	B	C	Choice
*4 × 25				
4 × 50				

	A + B	A + C	B + C	A + B + C
4 × 25				
4 × 100				

Main Set 2: Build the Frame With Arms (900y/m)

Cues	A	Arms are extensions of your scapula
	B	Slide the scapula in the direction of travel
	C	Allow the scapula to take the fingernails forward as if touching something in front of you

Whole stroke repeats with breathing

When breathing, keep your focus on the cue and try not to change your focus to breathing.

*First 6 strokes no breathing

	A	B	C	Choice
*4 × 25				
4 × 50				

	A + B	A + C	B + C	A + B + C
4 × 25				
4 × 100				

Theme: Generate Forward Momentum

- **Level 1**
- **Main sets total distance: 1200y/m**

Main Set 1 (600y/m)

Cues	A	Open the gate
	B	Slide scapula forward
	C	Relax lower arm and hand

Drills: 1 length with each cue, probably 4 repeats in each length, stand up after each drill repeat.

A	
B	
C	
Choice	

Short whole stroke repeats: 6 whole strokes, no breathing, stand up, repeat to end of length.

4 × 4 × 25	Rep 1	Rep 2	Rep 3	Rep 4
A				
B				
C				
Choice				

Whole stroke repeats with breathing

When adding breathing, keep your focus on the cue and try not to change your focus to breathing.

2 × 4 × 25	A	B	C	Choice
First 6 strokes no breathing, rest of length add breathing				
Breathing for the entire length				

Main Set 2 (600y/m)

Cues	A	Elbow out
	B	Tattoo forward
	C	Hit the cuckoo position

Drills: 1 length with each cue, probably 4 repeats in each length, stand up after each drill repeat.

A	
B	
C	
Choice	

Short whole stroke repeats: 6 whole strokes, no breathing, stand up, repeat to end of length.

4 × 4 × 25	Rep 1	Rep 2	Rep 3	Rep 4
A				
B				
C				
Choice				

Whole stroke repeats with breathing

When adding breathing, keep your focus on the cue and try not to change your focus to breathing.

2 × 4 × 25	A	B	C	Choice
First 6 strokes no breathing, rest of length add breathing				
Breathing for the entire length				

Theme: Generate Forward Momentum
- **Level 2**
- **Main sets total distance: 1600y/m**

Main Set 1 (800y/m)

Cues	A	Open the gate
	B	Slide scapula forward
	C	Relax lower arm and hand

Whole stroke repeats with breathing

When breathing, keep your focus on the cue and try not to change your focus to breathing.

*First 6 strokes no breathing

	A	B	C	Choice
*4 × 25				
4 × 25				
4 × 50				
4 × 25				

	A + B	A + C	B + C	A + B + C
4 × 25				
4 × 50				

Main Set 2: (800y/m)

Cues	A	Elbow out
	B	Tattoo forward
	C	Hit the cuckoo position

Whole stroke repeats with breathing

When breathing, keep your focus on the cue and try not to change your focus to breathing.

*First 6 strokes no breathing

	A	B	C	Choice
*4 × 25				
4 × 25				
4 × 50				
4 × 25				

	A + B	A + C	B + C	A + B + C
4 × 25				
4 × 50				

Theme: Generate Forward Momentum
- **Level 3**
- **Main sets total distance: 1800y/m**

Main Set 1 (900y/m)

Cues	A	Open the gate
	B	Slide scapula forward
	C	Relax lower arm and hand

Whole stroke repeats with breathing

When breathing, keep your focus on the cue and try not to change your focus to breathing.

*First 6 strokes no breathing

	A	B	C	Choice
*4 × 25				
4 × 50				

	A + B	A + C	B + C	A + B + C
4 × 25				
4 × 100				

Main Set 2 (900y/m)

Cues	A	Elbow out
	B	Tattoo forward
	C	Hit the cuckoo position

Whole stroke repeats with breathing

When breathing, keep your focus on the cue and try not to change your focus to breathing.

*First 6 strokes no breathing

	A	B	C	Choice
*4 × 25				
4 × 50				

	A + B	A + C	B + C	A + B + C
4 × 25				
4 × 100				

Endless Pool™

Theme: Build the Frame

- **Level 2**
- **Main sets total distance approx: 1600y/m**

Set the pool current to a level that allows you to stay in roughly the same place in the pool for a swim of up to a minute, with a moderate effort level.

Use a tempo trainer, underwater clock, or Endless Pool™ app to manage the duration of each repeat.

Main Set 1: Build the Frame No Arms (800y/m)

Cues	A	Head to foot alignment (feel tall, tilt pelvis if necessary)
	B	Release the head (turn off the muscles in the back of the neck so the head floats in a neutral position)
	C	Inside of elbows resting on rib cage

Whole stroke repeats with breathing

When breathing, keep your focus on the cue and try not to change your focus to breathing.

*First 6 strokes no breathing

	A	B	C	Choice
*4 × 30 secs				
4 × 30 secs				
4 × 60 secs				
4 × 30 secs				

	A + B	A + C	B + C	A + B + C
4 × 30 secs				
4 × 60 secs				

Main Set 2: Build the Frame With Arms (800y/m)

Cues	A	Arms are extensions of your scapula
	B	Slide the scapula in the direction of travel
	C	Allow the scapula to take the fingernails forward as if touching something in front of you

Whole stroke repeats with breathing

When breathing, keep your focus on the cue and try not to change your focus to breathing.

*First 6 strokes no breathing

	A	B	C	Choice
*4 × 30 secs				
4 × 30 secs				
4 × 60 secs				
4 × 30 secs				

	A + B	A + C	B + C	A + B + C
4 × 30 secs				
4 × 60 secs				

Theme: Generate Forward Momentum

- **Level 2**
- **Main sets total distance approx: 1600y/m**

Set the pool current to a level that allows you to stay in roughly the same place in the pool for a swim of up to a minute, with a moderate effort level.

Use a tempo trainer, underwater clock, or Endless Pool™ app to manage the duration of each repeat.

Main Set 1 (800y/m)

Cues	A	Open the gate
	B	Slide scapula forward
	C	Relax lower arm and hand

Whole stroke repeats with breathing

When breathing, keep your focus on the cue and try not to change your focus to breathing.

*First 6 strokes no breathing

	A	B	C	Choice
*4 × 30 secs				
4 × 30 secs				
4 × 60 secs				
4 × 30 secs				

	A + B	A + C	B + C	A + B + C
4 × 30 secs				
4 × 60 secs				

Main Set 2: (800y/m)

Cues	A	Elbow out
	B	Tattoo forward
	C	Hit the cuckoo position

Whole stroke repeats with breathing

When breathing, keep your focus on the cue and try not to change your focus to breathing.

*First 6 strokes no breathing

	A	B	C	Choice
*4 × 30 secs				
4 × 30 secs				
4 × 60 secs				
4 × 60 secs				

	A + B	A + C	B + C	A + B + C
4 × 30 secs				
4 × 60 secs				

Appendix 2

References

Chapter 2

Ericsson, K. A., and Pool, R. (2016). *Peak: Secrets From the New Science of Expertise*, London: Vintage, Quote adapted from p85.

Chapter 6

https://www.encyclopedia.com/science-and-technology/physics/physics/streamline, Accessed 2nd December 2023, Definition of Streamline.

Chapter 8

https://www.swimwellblog.com/archives/1132/, accessed 4th December 2023, Bill Boomer quote.

Chapter 10

https://www.openwaterpedia.com/wiki/Early_Vertical_Forearm, accessed 17th December 2023, Image of Early Vertical Forearm

Chapter 13

https://www.popularmechanics.com/military/a2126/4223354/, accessed 11th December 2023, Navy Seals research.